In Time of Flood

The Somerset Levels - The River Parrett

Poetry by James Crowden
Photography by George Wright

The Parrett Trail Partnership

Westover Bridge, Muchelney

For Nell, who occasionally lets me use the word processor
Sue, who looks after me in between times
and Tess, who knows the rivers and ditches far better than I do

First published in September 1996 by The Parrett Trail Partnership
South Somerset District Council, Brympton Way, Yeovil, Somerset BA20 2HT

Text © James Crowden 1996
Photographs © George Wright 1996
All Rights Reserved

ISBN 1 899983 25 2

A C.I.P. copy of this book is available at the British Library

Designed by Foothold
Printed by Wincanton Print

This book was written, designed, printed and published entirely in Somerset

Contents - Poetry

Acknowledgements

The poems have been collected over the last ten years and I am grateful to all those who have given of their time, information and support. Without their encouragement and criticism 'In Time of Flood' would not have surfaced.

Working with George Wright has been marvellous, and our trips, lurking around finding people and places, have been one of the chief delights. His pictures speak for themselves and tell their own story. I am also very grateful to Simon Barber of Foothold for his time, patience and expertise in the layout department.

At an early stage The Parrett Trail Project became interested and gave their support. Many thanks to Ralph Lister, Peter Milner, Paul Greatorex and Mark Etherington.

For help with funding the photography I am grateful to South West Arts, Wessex Water's Watermark Scheme, the Environment Agency, and one charity that wished to remain anonymous.

Thanks also to John and Lizzie Leach, Nick Rees, Michael Brown, Keith Budden, Evie Body, Robert Dunning, John Trevilian, Julian Temperley, H. M. Customs and Excise, Humphrey Temperley, Geoff Langford, David Boobyer, Nigel Hector, Serena de la Hey, Chinks Grylls, John Wealthy and Faith Needle, Lucy Willis and Tony Anderson, Peter Irvine, Chris Siddaway, Nick Sloane, Ray Harvey, Iain Sturdy, Peter Hart, Brendan Sellick, Crispin Aubrey, Ian Dunbar, James Palmer, Jenni Harrison, John Fletcher, Mary Carstairs, Chloe Fraser, Chris Chapman (Dartmoor) and Chris Chapman (Ilminster).

James Crowden, July 1996

The River Parrett Trail Project

The River Parrett Trail is a footpath from source to mouth, linking the south coast to the Bristol Channel. The trail takes the walker from the springs at Chedington in Dorset through some of the most interesting and attractive parts of Somerset, encompassing an Iron Age Hill Fort, as well as Stoke St Gregory, the centre of Somerset's basket making industry. Also included are the towns of Langport and Bridgwater, once important ports. The tide still reaches Oath, over 20 miles inland. The Trail finishes at Steart, a haven for wildfowl in winter.

The Parrett Trail Project however, is not just a footpath, but an on-going sustainable project that works with individuals and groups of people within the community. The aim is to explore and express the many different aspects of the river and its landscape, whether it be a village festival, a school exhibition, a new bridge, or a book of poems and photographs. We hope that each in its own way contributes to our understanding of this rich and fascinating landscape which has been reclaimed over the last thousand years. Above all it is the living, working nature of this area which is so vividly depicted in the words of James Crowden and the photographs of George Wright.

'In Time of Flood' captures the spirit of the Levels and Moors perfectly, and takes the reader on a fascinating journey down the Parrett from source to mouth, 'wriggling like an eel'.

Peter Milner, River Parrett Trail Co-ordinator, August 1996

Introduction

Water always has the power to intrigue us. From the earliest age we are fascinated by it. A child's view of a river is no different from that of an old sage. Even when we cannot see it we can feel it and rarely are unmoved by the sound of running water. Springs and waterfalls are obvious, but what about water before it comes to the surface? Why is it that we still have that strange ability to dowse for water and discover it hundreds of feet down? Either it is some kind of archaic survival mechanism which we used as hunters, gatherers and nomads, or it is simply our mind becoming re-attuned to the natural world around us. The re-forging of these deep links, return to the land, in whatever form, has become a major part of our life today, and one which we ignore at our peril.

Rivers have a hidden language. They are more or less a law unto themselves. Maybe it is no coincidence that the world's great 'civilizations' that pioneeered urban living all grew up alongside large rivers. The Nile, the Euphrates, the Tigris, the Indus, the Ganges, the Yangtse. The one thing they all have in common is that they flood regularly and their water can be used for intensive agriculture and the silt used to naturally fertilise their fields. Each river has its own characteristics and it can take quite a while to get a feel for the water in all its various moods. I was brought up on the edge of Dartmoor, and the rivers there left a very deep impression, fast and free flowing, hurrying to get down to the sea. The rivers of South Somerset are the very opposite. They take a pride in their sluggishness, and at times barely seem to move at all.

The River Parrett rises just into Dorset below Winyard's Gap. There are many springs and the village of Chedington is riddled with them. For the Celts these were always very important not just for watering animals and villages but as an 'eye', an opening into the 'Other world'. As a symbol for this I have used the design from a Celtic bronze mirror dug up in Dorset on a farm where I go sheep shearing. I saw it last year and I use it here to symbolically represent the Past, the pre-Christian realms of belief that are more in tune with the natural worlds than the scientific 'other' world of today. A world that at the mouth of the Parrett has left not only the brickworks and a plastics industry, but an explosives factory and a nuclear power station.

The Parrett was a formidable natural barrier, particularly in winter, and for a time provided a fluid boundary between the Celtic world and the Anglo-Saxon forces. The flooding kept them at bay. A divide between two minds and two languages. But more important than that, the Parrett was a trade route to Wales and beyond, a living corridor, a sinuous link in time from the world of the Celtic mirror to the world of the nuclear age. And down it flows the whole history of Somerset, from eels to helicopters, withies to cellophane, elvers to explosives. Taking in on the way, cider, woad, Cheddar cheese, teasles, flax and linen, rope and sail, bricks and tiles, King Alfred, the Battle of Sedgemoor and The Bloody Assizes, the Glastonbury festival, slime batches, hippies and travellers. A history rich in ferment and individual non-conformity. A non-conformity echoed by the natural world itself.

The distinctivness of the Somerset Wetlands, the Moors and Levels, is not always easy to capture. It changes from day to day. The flooding is not always predictable. These poems, these writings, notes and glimpses, are a mixture of observation and that history, a weaving together, the sense of working, the feel of the river and the intermeshed lives of those that live along its banks. Indeed the Parrett is not just one river but four. Three others flow into it - the Isle, the Yeo and the Tone, and one flows out - the Sowy river, which was constructed in the nineteen-seventies. The Cary used to flow into the Parrett at Burrowbridge but now forms the King's Sedgemoor Drain, and rejoins the river system at Dunball Wharf.

I have tried to grasp the subject as accurately as I can and would like to make a case for 'documentary' poetry which can be viewed in the same way as landscape or portrait painting. In some places I have experimented with various styles and rhythms, from Anglo-Saxon alliteration and half lines, to a more modern style bordering on rap and haiku. Not a few of the poems are printed in two or more sections, alongside each other. These can be read either individually or by switching from one side to the other, using two voices. This arose from the need to edit and fillet the longer, heavier poems and what emerged were new forms, new phrases, and new combinations, so I have left them open and breathing. Poetry should be capable of tackling large canvases, just as the Impressionists did a hundred years ago, and if you can do it with the Parrett, the slimiest river in Europe, you can do it with anything.

'In Time of Flood', like my earlier work, 'Blood Earth & Medicine', has an underlying theme not unrelated to anthropology. It is a study of people and places, a 'hunter-gatherer' way of life, that is unusual in this century of pensions, company cars and jet set travel. But more than that, this book goes beyond those boundaries. Ancient Taoists and Hindus knew a fair bit about the power and energy of rivers. The belief that the rivers are the source of life itself, is central to their prayers and contemplations. Maybe one day Bridgwater will become as holy as Benares, and there will be bathing ghats...

Often it is the hidden beauty and the quirkiness that makes the Wetlands what they are, and keeps people on their toes. A fluidity that has been captured perfectly by the eye and camera of George Wright, whose photographs tell their own story. We have chosen the less obvious pictures, the ones that give an interesting slant, that have the texture of smoked eel and Temperley's hooch; the stubborn individualism, the lurking rebelliousness which floats just beneath the surface. All that survival and swamp dwelling tucked beneath the belt.

But flooding, however scenic, is not always beneficial and can cause a fair bit of disruption for farmers and their wives. Animals drown, grass is ruined and if the flood's in your front room and rising, you know the damp course doesn't work. Quite a few cars are written off each year, like the one on the cover. The Underkeeper was lucky to escape alive. He now has a boat.

If you visit the area, please respect the privacy of those who live and work there. Enjoy the space, the freedom, the wildfowl... duck pâté.

James Crowden, July 1996

Naming the Parrett

From the eighth century onwards, the shifting tongue,

"Pedredistrem, Pedridan, Pedredan, Pedryd, Peret,
Pederydan, Pedredan, Pedret, Peret, Paret,
Perret, Pereith, Perreth, Peder, Parret...
Reached at long last circa 1575. with one **t**"

The first **dr** became an **rr**, and the second **d** a **t**, the **e** an **a**.
The curious running on of language, the twists and turns
The small shifts slowly became embedded, caught fast,
Anchored in the mind, tongue's legacy,
Dialect written down, fossilised on parchment.

And then there are the villages :
Sutpetret, Nortpetret, Sudperetonne, Norperton, Poderton, Porreton,
Which in turn became, without much trouble
South Perrott, North Perrott, South Petherton and North Petherton.

As to origin and meaning, there is some evidence,
From the Welsh and Cornish, leading to a tentative hypothesis.
Pedair, pedr = four; Rit meaning flow,
So in this case the four 'flows' or 'streams' are:
Tone, Yeo, Isle and Parrett.

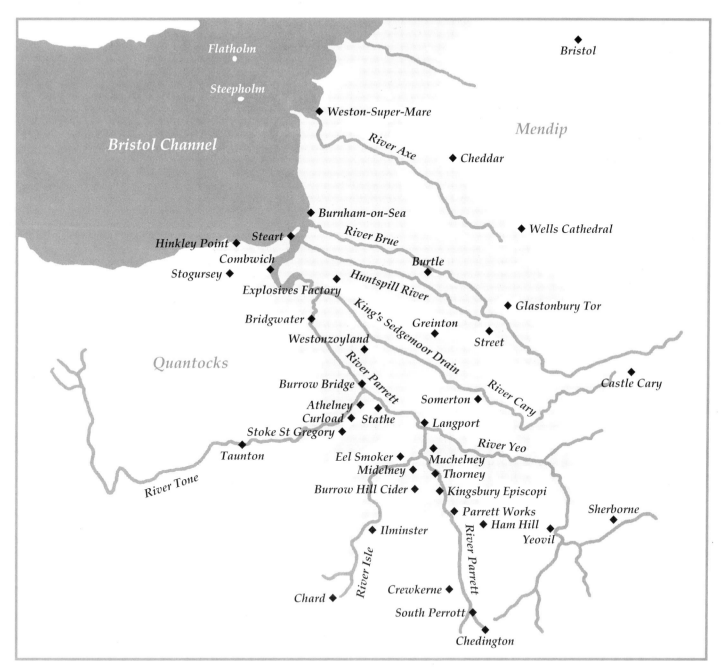

Celtic Mirror - River's Mouth

Curved
Strange patterns
Ignite the eye, unearthed,
Shadow's haunting, Celtic swirl
Playing games with the future, shamanic mask.
The glint carried down the centuries, fuelling our curiosity,
A diverse cult, hidden energy, the source of life itself, reflected
In the torchlight, engraved, the power to possess, power to name, a vital source,
A key to turn the spirit's grasp, unshackled for a moment, the 'Otherworld' beckoning
Running seawards, like a silver eel migrating, the heart of the river, the four flows
Winding down to the conger-salmon-mouth, treacherous with sand, mud and tide,
The way in on the bore, a sea flowing, sea moor kind of place.
Good for a surprise raid, if you like that sort of thing
And have guts. A tribal swamp with summer
Grazing. A green land, a rich land,
A place of fat cattle,
Sheep, geese
Cider.

Look at the stream and you will see the source
Look at the source and you will see the ocean

Drawing by Chloe Fraser

13

Source - Winyard's Gap & Chedington

Rising in the hills	not one source, but many
The ridge, a scarp	a gap, a hub
A horseshoe	where two backbones meet
Filleted and slender	ancient pivot
An amphitheatre	village and field
Colonised with beech	skyline of hillfort and lookout
Old belief	keyed in with tribal complexity
Gnarled root	strange ditch
Imprint of rampart	a place where water is shed
Shed and parted	from one coast to another
Three ways mingled	below the ridge
The gap where the water comes	each spring
An underground maze	a hidden path
A pilgrimage to the light	a gurgling pattern
In times of drought	men would have killed for
Fluid marvel	deep resonance
Music within the hill	that rare commodity
High water and grazing	the Celtic prayer
Rising up out of the bed rock	a place of offering
Steep clefts	riven and slippery
Eye of the flood	first innocent trickle
Birth of a river	in a grove of hazel
Slender	the silver messenger
Nuzzling the earth	leaf mould
Gully run	ooze beneath the bramble.

Chedington Court Gardens

Flowers by phone, Chedington

Early Stages - South Perrott

Stream feeds stream	a welter of small rivulets
Faint offerings	web of ditches
Each brook	a babbling strand
Spun yarn	constant thread
Twisted	plied together
Old landscape	stitched in tightly
Each farm	each catchment
A small tuck	a fretsaw of hedges
Interlocked and woven	the lie of the land
The run off	the waterbasin
A family affair	shepherded on down
The water bridged	abutted
Measured	marvelled at
Ushered on	first house
First village	the settlement clustered
Nestled in the hollow	first bridge
Traffic...	almost unnoticed
The language of fluidity	channeled
Contained	river runs on
Taut and dark	strong as a ship's hawser.

Mountain Bikes, Ham Hill

Ham Hill

From here you see it all   nose to tail, source to mouth
The whole history of Somerset   wriggling like an eel
Invisibly winding   a fair slice
From assart to turbary   from Alfred's jury to Judge Jeffreys
Parcelled and apportioned   hope on the end of a pitchfork
Non-conformity and dissent   retribution with a goose quill
Hung, drawn and quartered   boiled in brine
The last Rebellion salted down   half a bushel each
Two fingers at Parliament   Monarchy and the Army

"Bring in ye next prisoner... let us see his rascally face"
"Don't waste ye courts time... by pleading ye innocence"

From here you see it all   from squash court to converted barn
Council house to factory door   powered flight to Hinkley Point
Hamlets gobbled up by urban pike   the hotchpotch of fields
Rich land, poor land   glebe land, duchy land
Plough land, cabbage land   maize and corn
Potato, dairy and beef   linseed, rape and kale
Apples and blackcurrants   sheep, tomatoes, silage and setaside.

"The love of fair play and justice... is in the very marrow of my bones"

Land that once grew rigging flax and hemp for rope and sail
Tamed the wind powered the seven seas
Now sprouts greenhouses hooters and glove factories
Dual carriageways Roman Emperors would have been proud of
Diners and dog kennels helicopters and police stations
Off licences and video shops lottery outlets and ice cream vans
Travellers camps notices to quit
Bubblers and lurchers fluttering in the wind
Old railway lines canoodling
Late at night young lovers
In the carpark entwined on the back seat
The whole history of Somerset trouble with ye gear stick...

Ray Harvey's Quarry

Ham Hill Stone

Quarried

Out of pockmarked hill

The amphitheatre

Drilling rigs and diggers

An opera played out

Jurassic sea life regurgitated

Remembered, fossilised

Spawning villages

Towns and bridges

The silent audience

Countless houses

Churches, chapels and schools

Roof shingles and staddlestones

Flagstones and fireplaces

Dovecotes and gravestones

Coaching Inns and pubs

Old cider houses and tithe barns

Abbeys and County courts

Asylums, mills and lock ups

The libretto of warm stone

Yellow and soft to touch

Preserved with preservation orders

Trellised, embellished

Revered and championed like W.I. jam

steep

and lingering

wedged

filleted

the ring of chisel

hammer echo

tungsten tip

cutting

through

rock

the air

sliced thin

like salami

multiplied

a clean face

manhandled

levered

on rollers

eased back

the circular

saw

dripping

cooled

exultant.

Ben: the Primary Saw

Ramblings - Sluice and Weir

Steadied like a dog at heel
Reed winding and sluggish
Water crickets
Water-lily and flag iris
Alive with dragonflies
Soon-to-be-chopped-down
Flickering
A green edged ripple
Staunch trunks rustle
A chorus within
Gathers pace as it nears
Curved and fluid
From one world to another
A dark avenue
The following of the wall
Into the light
Each weir, each sluice
Each wheel and ratchet
To his advantage
The sudden letting go
The river's muscle
Still rippling
Dark sanctuary

curved water
reverberating
pondskaters
whirligigs
damsel flies
groves of bat willow
light and shade
running
a powerful cathedral
that gathers pace
the sluice and weir
as if pouring
the steps alive
between the trees
running on downstream
slow swallowing up
patient hanging back
simple mechanism
a mill race
fresh energy flushed
flexed and taut
in the half light
like an eel squirms

ox-bowed and cow laden
with water boatmen
arrowhead and frogbit
the hushed air floating
gnats and caddis
a last silent flutter
river of leaves
between sky and grazing
light and sound carrying
only stumps remain
sudden sliding over
from an enormous jug
the river's voice
hidden cloister
brief emergence
the bridge's arch
carved against sky
that man can turn
powerful and daunting
in its fluid fury
reined in
reassumes its pace
and squirms again.

Parrett Weir

Revolutionary Lettering

The Parrett Works

Solid and substantial
A place where machines were born
Where water powered their desire
The slavery of cogs and shuttles
A place where flax and hemp
Where coal and steam shaped
Chimney powered
A haven for invention
The old owners long since legged it
Flax for muskets
The old fool proof equation

a temple to Victorian ingenuity
worshipped and assembled
to conquer the world of raw materials
honed down, the ratio of this and that
turned into sail and rope
forged and fired the imagination
an Ironbridge in miniature
with an elegant weir, sluice and eel trap
down under with dolphins and Maoris
desire and disease
colonial appetites and sea-whaling

And now, a century later
The vast wheel still waiting
Fine letters are cut
Carving silence out of rock
The language of form
Translating words
The eye entrenched
On the printed page
Invisible between the lines
Heidelberg and Monotype
Leading to the computer room

long muzzled
like an actor out of work
chisel on clean stone
flecks of light
spaced and flowing
precise art
arrests the mind
the history of typography
hot lead and fork lifts
the next generation
circular staircase, ground coffee.

The Proprietor, Parrett Works

Nick's Kitchen

Burrow Hill Cider Farm

There in the barn dark

Inch by inch

The steady inquisition

The confession extracted

As the press pushes home

Flows ever more freely

Ruddy brown and golden

A river in flood

Whole orchards

The never ending tide

Ebbing and flowing

Mounds of apples

Like long barrows

Lagoons of red and yellow...

Dabinett and Porter's Perfection

Bloody Turk, Yarlington Mill

Tremlett's Bitter, Tom Putt

Their ransomed juice

Vast in their yeast brooding

Broad in the beam

Their froth fermenting bellies

Straps of iron, barrels

A Norman trick

Distilled and fiery

layer by layer

gallon by gallon

begins

bit by bit

life blood of the heathen apple

the stout cheese dripping

like honey

a hive of fruit

pulped and crushed

trailers

acres deep and rounded

tipped and spewed forth

the farmyard filled to bursting

Brown Snout and Chisel Jersey

Stoke Red, Kingston Black

Lambrook Pippin

Somerset Royal

pumped to distant vats

potent and powerful

fecund and fattening

bound with oak

giant and gargantuan...

this drink from apples

hint of orchard on the tongue...

Cider House Gang

Chris King moving apples

Spreading pomace

'the stout cheese dripping'

Washing down

The Spirit Level

The Somerset Cider Brandy Distillery

Josephine and Fifi · shipped in from Normandy
Side by side · circus of shining pipes
Vie with one another · sleek jungle
A brace of Calvados stills · copper columns, tangled
Tramp steamers · like an engine room in the tropics
Showing their age a little · resurrected, 'Fabrique en Paris'
One, large and reliable · the other small and fast
Like the au pair... · faithfully fermented
Distilled, condensed · the ship's log, a grubby chart
The longitude and latitude · navigating oceans of cider
Plotted, the orchard's wake · each rivet, each drop
Precious liquid · clocked and tamed
A symphony · hidden behind glass
The copper serpent · a cauldron refined
Hot, heady and powerful · yields up its nectar
Clear, aromatic · ardent and sensuous
Level spirit, eau-de-vie · avant-garde mystique.

Josephine, Fifi and Richard

The Spirit Bond

The Warehouse

Quiet reformatory,
biding time, twiddling thumbs
in the cool, damp, even darker dark.
Cooper's craft, committed, sectioned, curved,
caulked and tapped. A gallery of gargantuan
barrels, hogsheads stacked high, five score fuming
and fiery. Nurtured from blossom to bottle,
Dragon's bite held within oak like gunpowder
kegs about to explode. The Alternative
Communion, hours of reflection, seeking the right
nose. Strong, smooth and blended. Robust, full,
round and rebellious in body like teenagers
growing up, sleek as an otter, the spirit's path, an
inner glow, the Angel's share, the knowing
look. A Somerset trick, surreptitiously
smuggled down the ages,
a butt laid down.

'the Angel's share'

Shani Honeybun gives a taster

Another satisfied customer

Thorney Mill

Thorney Mill

Water

Wheel drips

Slow revolutions

Fluid energy held back

Tapped, only half controlled

The river's arc begins to pulse

Pulling and pursued, a vast force

Runs through the building, judders

Turns stone, turns wheat into flour

Dark-hidden and silent, unleashed

The power of the water, river's voice

Grinding grain, vast cogs intermesh

Slow majesty of such machinery

Delight and danger, trapdoors

Gape, strong arm of the river

Flexing augers and hoists

Musty hessian, West

Of England sacks

Grainbins

Flour

Last mill on the Parrett or the first,
if you are coming up stream
with a barge. Mill pool
swirling dark and
deep. The wheel
house covered
in moss like
some old
Japanese
shrine.

Everywhere pale hanging
Early morning mist, white faces peer
Cough and splutter, the vibrancy
A gamelan orchestra rippling out across the moor...

Carp	Kingfisher
Vast and brooding	A glit of blue
Sun themselves	A scud in the gloaming
In the shallows	Close to, a near thing
Swim lazy	Vivid
Turn and circle	Darts over the weir
Glide, hang	The catching
And then hover	The acrobatics of it all
Glean and clean	The flight
Filter the water	Tight like a spitfire
Feed and loaf	Zips
Scales glisten	And waggles its wings
Lips twitch	Only niftier
Fin, gill and tail	Feather-flight
Mark time	Blue-green streak
Meditate	Half seen in the dusk
On the flow	Dips and dives
Hide under leaves	Searches and perches
Of arrowhead	Low, so low
The size of the beast	Fast food
Haunting the water	On the water's rim
Sumo wrestler	The insects...
Of the millpond.	... the insects.

Sculpture 45

The Bishop

Somerset Light - Autumn

Somerset light	sleek and slanting
Skewers orchards and gates	wriggles under barbed wire
Pierces old farmhouses	barns
Old glass	slewing each mottled shaft
Mullioned windows	slip and slide
Low September	late the afternoon lapping
Dappled and dancing	backing and advancing
Glancing	through the apple tree
Mute shadows	flickering leaves
Thin veins of energy	edge and etch their way forward
Alive and ecstatic	pulse and ripple
A ripe stream reflected	the sun's wake
A silent symphony	juggling the light's laughter
Sacred	the sense of season drawing in
End grain encompassed	flame returning
Evening ellipse	illuminated
Hamstone and oak panel	open hearth, ash and embers
Re-kindled	first smoke, first fire.

Somerset Light - Winter

Somerset light	murky in the mist brooding
Sullen and damp	winter's mantle
The shroud	its invisible spell cast
A shawl	binding moors and levels
A solitary fastness	a thick blanket
Within which people move	slow and sluggish
Tarnished by its vapour	seeping into their joints
Struggling	the rising damp
To meet the midday sun	to penetrate the veil
A faint halo	half-hovering over ditches
Rivers, rhynes, and runnels	islands
Connected by thin causeways	thin slice of cattle-breeding land
Fuelling the flatness	uneasy and unrepentant
The ghosts of withy trees	caught between water and mist
Marsh-memory lingering still	a quirkiness settling in

The solemn grey pulse... out of which only the heron rises.

Heron Fishing - Heron Rising

Silent and stealthy sleek	steely still, beady eyed
Narrow neck craned and tufted	the dapper dandy
Poised above the ripple	hidden in the reeds
Sly sentinel	monocled hunchback
Vain admirer of his own reflection	lurks like sculpture
About to move	fleet and stabbing
The sharp punishing blade	darts
Fractures the water	pinions its prey
Swift purpose	gulps and gulps again...

Grey merging with sky... swallows silver on the green bank

Long and lanky, the Fisher King	legs it like a stork
Undercarriage trailing	ungainly, gawky
Hefty wings massage the air	rises up
As if casually, patrols	its kingdom
Back alleys and damp waterways	ditches interlaced
The shamanic realm	sky and water
Slowly sauntering seawards	bends of sluggish rivers
Slippery and slimey	oozey eel-laden mud
Half hidden in tidal sludge	surfaces from the depths
The dark low, slow flow	of the soft, flat, fat land
Still wriggling within the belly	last in-flight meal.

Woodstack, Muchelney Pottery

Nick Rees and the wood kiln

John Leach's Pottery at Muchelney

Throwing	Firing the Wood Kiln	Unloading
Raw clay	Sparks fly	Days later
Pushed and coaxed	Ash falls	The uneasy
Weighed, pummelled	Sweat and heat mingle	Prising apart
Squeezed, delved into	Skin glistens	Expectation
Thrown again	A firm bank of fire	Like opening
Cajoled into shape	Feeding the chamber	An Egyptian tomb
Wet, the steady flow	Shed's shadows	Oddity confirmed
Between canny fingers	Hemmed in behind bricks	Felt and admired
Revolving	The flame's pulse	Succulent curve
Mug, jug	A healthy glow	Watching
Pot and flagon	Bursts and erupts	The master's eye
Dish, plate	The beast alive	Held in the hand
Vase and cup	The Dragon's tongue	Moored like a barge
Roundness secured	Devouring all before it	The quayside
Form levelled	Wicked dance	Customs inspection
And evening	Shapely cargo	The trestle table
Eye's grasp	Red, orange, yellow	A wharf
Pedalling the wheel	Incandescent white	Heat lingering
Powering the shelves	Volcanic and tempestuous	As if somehow
A silent army	Voyage of heat	We have witnessed
Chinese warriors	Flames' harvest	A miracle
Wait for the kiln.	Glaze begins to drip.	The first rising of bread.

'oddity confirmed'

On the road to Drayton

Perry Moor Rhyne

In Time of Flood - The River Parrett

Rain and river run	wild waters rise, rebellious
Succulent and sinuous	each sensuous bend
Winding its way seaward	curved currents brim
Heady in hidden depths	brown banks burst their bodice
Merge and overspill	breathe more freely, let go in reams
The heavy water's cargo	swift in silt
Slowly seeping	draws the land down, sodden and submerged
Steeped and stored	sprawled and spread, the temper eased
Wanders dark and quivering	between the withy beds
Rhynes held hostage	a silent shallow haunting
Without a ripple	the flood's quiet carpet runs for miles
A strange mirror	held up to the eye
Polished and poised	the slice of light
The water's sheen-shimmer	skimming rank sedge
Reed-rustled and ruckled	the reflected light-dazzle
Strewn and scattered	sudden furious flurry of small waves
Weaving and weary-worn	slither of silver meadows
A shining shawl of pearls	a shoal of fresh fish
Flung glittering in the gloaming	a glad glimmer
A gauntlet thrown down	the river's voice
The rain's torrid majesty	turbulent and tempestuous
The hidden pulse	pushing at walls and bridges
Sluices and weirs in full pelt	nudging towns and trees
The flood's free measure	rampant and flowing

Each gate   fuelled by further distant downpours
An inland sea   a window through which the light slides
Where the river meets the sky   the scudding source
Sharp and clear, stark and gaunt   sunken,the winter ground
Pollarded and punctuated   stumps of withy, sore thumbs
Hoisted on the horizon   silhouetted and silent
Like witnesses after an execution   the land drowned
The sky stretched and stretching   taught like a canvas
A staunch saddle   over which geese wheel.

Overleaf: Muchelney 'In Time of Flood'

Wildfowl on West Moor

In flood by Pitt bridge / the Main Drain awash and swamped
One step more, and then, aghast / the sudden flight rises
Manic, the swerving orchestra / on the wind's wing
Ricochet, screech and wheel / jive and manoeuvre
The city of wildfowl / winter and wait, watch, wary
Wily and wise to ways of the water / seen but not heard
Heard but not seen / circumspect commuters
Committed to the wetland / a score of swans, solid and sumptuous
Run on the water / rise up like old flying boats
Creak and lumber, heeled hard over / slowly gain their height
Careen, curved necks outstretched / white wings weave improbable circles
Each arc, a lost language / empowered by its own reflection
Form, fluidity, fuelled and fused / a flowing that the water has shaped
Secured, safe haven / surrendering to the sky
Theirs and theirs alone / a right to throng and thrive
Pitch and dive / flotillas of widgeon and teal
Shoveller and pintail / lapwing, redshank, plover and snipe
Mallard and moorhen / ruff and warbler
Each wing wielding its own flight / plight and purpose
Each cunning strategy / woven into the water's edge
A measure of secrecy / honed down into the habitat
Winter's withy beds, a shield / welcome, fluty and reedy
Low eerie whistle, curlew calling / delicate like gossamer
A silvery slither / hanging in the thin air
Each thrilling note / threading the dusk's mantle.

Counting Cormorants

Winter Levels

Perched astride the seasons	the hand of man
Hovered long	compromise and revolt
A deal struck long ago	two worlds
Territory shared	like two brothers
Fighting it out	ever since
The damp inheritance	only half reclaimed
Week by week	month by month
Year by year	they wrestle it out
High land and low land	wet land and dry land
Summer and winter	field by field
Inch by inch	sheep and cattle
Foot by foot	driven to safety
Roads and farms	sink without trace
The damp oozes everywhere	casts an invisible web
Each hollow	links old marsh
Like reading a wrinkled palm	old rivers half sunken
A glistening slate	the inland sea
Pumped and pursued	sharp boundaries
Thin strips	arrows of light
Thin veins of a vast leaf	each flood notched up
Like children	on the kitchen door
Drowned sheep	furniture awash, pigs in trees
Banks burst	creeping upstairs
The village underwater	the smell of sewage
Rowing boats	tied to the bedroom window.

Muchelney Abbey

Frozen, frozen, heavy frosts impound the sky, doubley trapped

The same land a water-sheen withy pool, pale ransom

Cloak of rime wrapped tight white on white, opaque

A subtle sheet that contours each sunken fallow field

Each level segment of sedge marooned moor, caught and held fast

Rhyne by rhyne silent and sullen

The chain linked and lined long wavering regiments

Reeds and bulrushes slender lances that pierce the ice shadow

Hostages stiffly surrendering cruel siege of cold air

An island refuge a place of meditation

Caught between the rising sun the full moon of prayer

Abbot's grazing acres of mist and hoar frost

Sheep's breath, each smeech powering the dim light

Their befuddled forms faintly visible, shrouded buildings

Outlined, crystalised ice and vapour mounting

The sense of memory lingering, fostered, triggered off

An earlier order of things a litany of sharp light

The shaft appearing for that one brief moment

First warmth sun's voice breaking through

The veil penetrated prising apart the mist's mantle

Pursues dim shadows showers the fields

Illuminated the early morning manuscript

A swallet of golden light glistening

Gleaming the avalanche of ice-dazzle.

Another Early Morning, c 1520 AD.

Word has got around, goings on at the Abbey...

"... And not just new fire places either
All that food and just for twenty?
I say, there must be more there
And not all the same shape and size
And what was that about separate bedrooms?
All that rebuilding?
A place of seclusion all right
But whose paying for it I ask?"

"Whose paying for it? All that land
Why they've got Midelney, and Thorney as well
And what with the mill, they've got it all sewn up
Shouldn't be allowed, that's what I say
And as for people creeping back to their villages
Early in the morning... say no more
Women ought to know better
But when its frozen
And there's a little snow on the ground
You can follow their footprints
From back door to back door
The Abbot's grazing all right
But not just sheep, if you follow my meaning..."

The Priest's House

Through the lavender
A doorway emerges
As if in turning
The handle
Time's clasp
Has shed its grip
The inner light
Reverberating
At a slower pace
The passage of oak
Hamstone and blue lias
A slow communion of ideas
Interwoven
Beneath the wheat reed
A slow settling of joints
A chalice of woodwork
Passed down
Lurking, restored
Propped up
Waiting
For the next flood
Candles and candle light
The table sealed
Beeswax and turpentine.

Fishermen on West Sedgemoor

Slabs of water
Chunks of light
The rhyne embalmed
Embarked on
A sluggish journey
Its banks punctuated
Lone fishermen
Monks meditating
On their prayers
Everyday a Friday
Their silent incantations
Barbed and hooked
With bait, the solemn look
The green umbrella
Betraying not an ounce of hope
Their minds
Filled with past adventures
Measured in pounds and inches
The hours spent watching
Their own reflection
The rod's tremulous pulse
Eagerly awaited
The tug that confirms
That they are still alive.

The Priest Himself - December 1348

"Of course he had his meals   brought over from the Abbey
The Bishop of Bath & Wells   sorted that out
Laid it down in an ordinance   didn't he?
Like meals on wheels   meat twice a week
Fish on Fridays   eggs, a large loaf of bread daily
AND two gallons of ale   not bad for a cushy number"

But then there was no glebe land   the price of clergy
The cost of cloth   faith in a barrel
The annunciation measured out   wheat and malted barley
The abbey's obligation   keeping the villagers at bay
Up to the mark, belief in rotundity an outpost of Latin
Grace and Benediction   the burial party
The journey to the 'other world'   Black Death about to pounce
Only two months old   and roaming around Langport
Your Life Insurance policy   a plague of rats
The microbe in the flea gut   knotted at the waist
The package deal, promises to avert the fires of hell
Eternal damnation   the power to excommunicate
A protection racket   a place in the churchyard
Only a small price to pay   your salvation
The feeding and watering   one priest
Meat, bread, fish, firkins and flagons ale
Nunc Dimittis. Quicklime   Pax Vobiscum. Plague.

Midelney	The Underkeeper
An island in winter	Kept under, unkempt
Down by the bridge	Lucky to keep alive
The road's throat	Somehow managed
Cut by the old river	To escape from his car
Flowing	Not in a ditch
Through the hedge	But five feet of water
The Manor	Late one night
Falcon's mews	Taking a short cut
Safe	From Eli's over Black bridge
In their own estuary	Forgot it was flooded
Encircled	Huish Drove
Enveloped	Frogmen and the fire brigade
A moat of their own	Flying his hawk
Cattle	Redtailed buzzard
And people	Yellow claws
Driven in	Grip rabbit's heads
Geese and sheep	Neck of a pheasant
Safe from the flood	Plucked out of the air
Food stored up	Eyeball to feather celebrating
The heron's roost	Another trip to the cells
A perch in history.	A mean beast, preening itself.

The Coracle	*The Old Canoe*
Like a leaf	Dug out
Cowhide	Resurrected
Riding the river's swirl	Dark timber
Negotiating the bends	Hollowed
Each figure of eight	Almost shiny
A small twist	The trunk
Deft dab of the wrist	A legacy of peat
Sliding the paddle	Its length and breadth
The knack mastered	A learning curve
Hazel and ash interlocked	Capable of holding
Going on down the river	Many fish, or else
Nothing between you	The carcasses of deer
And the sea	Wild pig
Land slipping by	Simple solution
An ancient skill	Paddled out of the past
Spinning around	Curiosity
Walking on water	Stored behind glass
A temporary home	Beckons, excites
Carried aloft	Floats gently
The walnut shell, eclipsed.	In our imagination.

'An ancient skill'

At Midelney Pumping Station	Shearing at Greinton
Ugly, but there it is	No shade, nothing
Sixties, functional	Just a concrete yard
Glass, steel, electricity	Heat dancing, humid
State of the art	Like taking the cork off a bottle
Main drain held back	Sharp dogs
A weir, a lock, a grid	800 sheep driven in
Where the water has five levels	From the drove's end
Each with their own pace	Hot and panting
History swirling	Yolk well risen
Beneath the surface	Lanoline
Rivers meet like people meet	Clammy and close
Currents that tug, pull	King's Sedge
Divulge and diverge	Not a breath
Merge	Only swamp fever
Flow back on themselves	Unrelenting glare
Overspill	Keeling over
Turbulent in time of flood	Dry and drowsy
Converge	First signs
Sleek and brown	Neck burnt
Two heads glide	Balance gone, as if drugged
Seek the bulrushes	Blurred
A place where things happen	Fingers seize
And nothing happens	Heat stroke
Poplars rattle.	We shout for water.

Moors   *Meads Levels Rhynes Droves Sand Banks & Reaches*

West   South Curry Ten Foot Twelve Foot

Wick Wet   Aller Lang Eighteen Foot Two Mile Pedwell

Common Out   Whit Rod Port Hearty Mark Yeo Butleigh Beer Door

Land Row Hulk   Church East Shaking Dobbins Aller Second Fyddlers End

Perry Sutton   Compton Dundon Smed Kings Liberty Nidons Great Withy

Huish Walton   Haskey Stawell Godney Kennard Tadham Tealham Duck Pool

King's Sedge   Queen's Sedge Top   War Withy Pennard

Splotts Crannel   Stoke Gold Corner   Wedmore Westhay

Redlake Binham   Knowle Westbury   Cheddar Cripps

Draycot Kenn   Stock Sheepwash   Mark   Horlake Fore

Allerton Puxton   Edington Corn   Helland Burtle   Catcott Hay

Holly Ashcott   Purseys Mare   Somerton Door   Wet Crowds

Dry Crowds   Crab Hole   Earlake Pawlett   Ablake Sher

South Lake   Poolmead Lyng   Chedzoy Little

Witchey Greylake   Monk Little Hook   Huntspill Thorney

Sale Piece Langleaze Weston Pensoy Hammocks Crabtree   Stathe

Burrow Wall Beer Wall Shepherd's Rattling Bow   Bawdrip

Ninestreams Short Folkes Long Load Wagg   Turkey   Sedge

Middle Marchant's Sands Pitney Wick Oath   Swell   Pathe

Peaky Corner Old Works Aller Hamp   Stan

Black Hole Straight Crooked Middlezoy   Lower Salt

James Wear Elms Reach Low Ham Shapwick Goose Barry

Yellow Batches Higher Ropes Pimms Pill Pawlett Ketch

Lower Ropes Big Bend Horsey Cut Chisel Rocks

End of an Era

"Not the money in it like there used to be...
Why there used to be a hundred or more acres out there
All grown up, a proper factory we had here
The whole of Kingsbury was at it, but that died off
Like the coal coming up the river in barges
Then the railway went, and then the mill packed up
And then the milk factory. My father used to bring hay
From Hambridge over in a boat, in time of flood
Cut it with a hayknife to feed the cattle
End of an era now, we're on the building
Laying blocks at Broadwindsor, new thatched cottages
Course they want the willow hurdles for the gardens
Privacy and all that, but we just grubbed the old bed out
Demand is higher than ever
Suppose another few years time we'll have a grant
To put them back in again. Just a few bundles left
Taking them to Bournemouth for the blind
They can at least see the future"

Brian Howard talking about Westmoor leaning over a fence
By Thorney Mill, August 1995.

On the way to the Halfway House

Langport, c. 935AD

A hook, a bend in the river
The water twisted like an iron bar
Causeway and ford
Port and mint, frontier agreed
Barrier enough between the two worlds
Saxon and Celt
Still fighting it out
On Saturday nights
In various pubs
A silver penny would buy
Fodder for five horses
Bread for eight men
The daily pay of a soldier
Shearing of a score of sheep
Fourpence the sheep itself
But if any man cheated the king
Or minted his own money
Outside the port
One hand cut off
Nailed to the door
A warning, a reminder
Of Athelstan's decree
Index linked, the cost of living.

Battle of Langport, 1645

Uncertainty
Clouded
In a smeech
Squalls of hot horses
Gallivant and dally
Reluctant
In leather jerkins
Pikemen advance
Like clumps of bulrushes
Hedgehogs surging
Towards their deaths
Musket ball
Sabre cut
Cannon
Black powder
Etched
On their nostrils
Small reprieve
From thirst
The uphill charge
A daring move
That cost the King
The West Country.

Stuckey's Lock, Langport

The 'Gladstone'

Not much at first glance
Battered, somewhat dishevelled
Stained with creosote
That charts six years
Length 182' 1"
Breadth 34' 5" Depth 23' 8"
In the name of JW Bagehot
A fair vessel. an East Indiaman
Registered in Bridgwater, 1873
Bristol, Cardiff, London
Cochin, Colombo, Falmouth
Such expense as the Captain
Might incur. Port dues
Medicine, In and Out Pilotage
Captains' meal ashore £2-5-0
Potatoes and paddy
Ballast and shackles
Present for good management
Sails, butcher, miller
Telegrams to Langport and Colombo
Bazaar supplies
The sheaf of voyages
Conjured up, still reeking

the expense account
stored at Thorney Mill
precise, copperplate
in that vessels life
that 1" very important to Lloyds
tonnage 1057
Langport. Walter himself
built in 1860
Entries for Spain
Newcastle, Liverpool, Bombay
Montevideo, Rio, New Orleans
Mr Watson
tobacco and soap, the doctor
file for X cut saw 3/-
chandlery, stevedores
dunnage mats
yam and more potatoes
optician, wages, wire rope
more ballast, water
Bombay £2-11-6
entries, logged and dated
preserved in creosote
outlive the ship.

Kelways Nursery, Langport

Labels

In time of need

A Rastafarian takes a walk from Langport to Monk's Leaze Clyse

Old bridges, fridges   plastic bags
Bottles, barrels   bicycle frames
Fast food containers   aerosols
Lock gates locked   each valve chained up
Mechanism in   suspension, Man
Monk's Leaze Clyse   and Sowy river
Whiff of sewage   from sewage works
Buzz of a 125   sleek like an eel
Just escaped   from the capital
Buffet car   reflected teal
Moor blank faces   moorhen, swans
Twelve black cormorants   perching there
Aller Court   and Burrow Mump
The moors improved   like a swimming pool
One end deep   the other shallow
Don't let the NRA   catch you now
Diving off   is a terrible crime
Don't tamper   with the Levels Man
Don't you let that water go   hold it tight, like a good boy now
Don't want to flood   the old Bridgwater
Don't pull the plug   ain't finished my game
The moors is brown   the moors is flat
The moors is green   like a billiard table
Snooker, pool   Dig the peat. Moses
Don't pot the black stuff...   Now. Man.

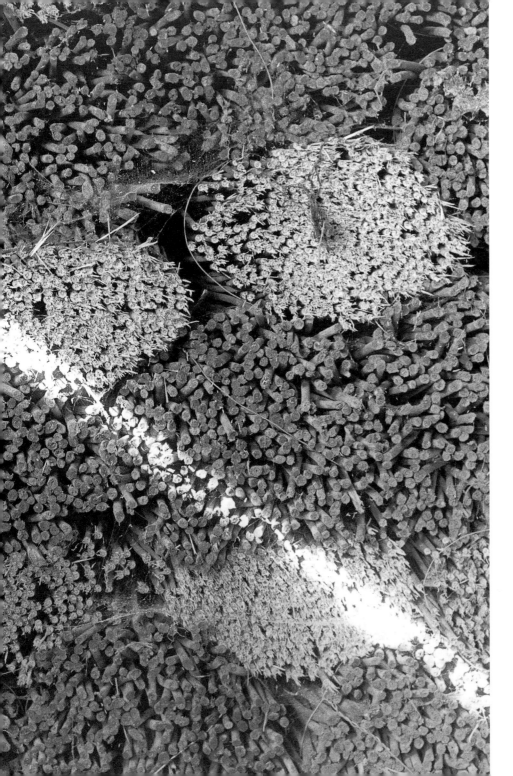

Withies (i)

Plant, harvest, cut and carry
Sort, boil, strip and tie
Harnessed for life
The withy beds
Work horse of the Wetlands
Colonies of sallow and osier
Tall forests
Tremulous and vibrant
Saddled
Shimmer above the water
A slender orchestra of rods
Weaving beneath the sky
A rattle of green light
Dappled percussion
Swaying in the breeze
Reflected
And quivering
Each breath
A deep resonace
Leaf-rustle
And shadow-dart
The supple river
Tidal surge far-rippling
Beyond the acre's boundary.

(ii)

Every foot
A slug of willow
Every two
A new row planted
Rigid wands
Cut short, shoved in
With the heel
Of the hand
Back bent and six abreast
The workers
Slow progress
The sullen line
A silent wavering army
Plods across the ploughed
And harrowed land
A small miracle, repeated
Tillered by cattle
Each bed a hive
Of industry
Lasting as long as any orchard
Each family
A small stake
Driven home
Into the wetland.

(iii)

Generations of sharp hooks
Have cut
Crouched and curved
A silver sickle
Half moon
Clasped in the hand
Deft and purposeful
Slick dab of the wrist
A thousand eyes
Staring up at you
Sleek the winter wind
Nubbing the small stumps
Eager to burst forth
Once more
Invisible and pliant
The power of the forest
Harvested
Carried home
High on shoulders
Each wad
Stacked and sorted
Stoutness drawn tight
Sealed with a rose knot
The bond of green withy.

(iv)

Black Maul
Black Spaniard
Champion Rod
Red, brown, buff
Almost orange
Half submerged
Yet buoyant
Dripping bundles
Fished out
Like some ancient craft
From the Euphrates
Steeped in long vats
Trod in by stalwart boots
Pungent and seeping
Sharp rank smell
Salicylic acid
Bark and tannin
The oily slick fuelled
By odds and ends
Coal and hedge trimmings
The boiling up
An intimate process
Like doing your own
Laundry in public.

Geoff Langford, Wick Moor

(v)

And then the stripping
Of the bark
In the dark low shed
The constant drum
Thud and drone
Surge and rattle
The acrid peel
The feel of pulling
Twist and turn
Shedding the skin
Like a viper
Revealing its flesh
Smooth
Yet taut and whippy
Supple and strong
Pliable, a humour
Turned in on itself
Wry and dry, easier now
Than it then was
Four pence a wad
And one at a time
Outside the garden shed
The stripping break
Women's work.

(vi)

Against the fence
Rods, spread out to dry
A brown river
A watery harvest
Sheaves of willow
Prized and pursued
By regiments
Of other hands
Hands that twist
Bend and weave
Tuck in and tuck under
The curved lattice
Interlocking
Hidden strength
Firm yet flowing
Rising from the floor
Slewing and randing
Stout fingers
Bid the willow
To take its new shape
Coaxed and bent
Thwacked home
Young shoots
For an old purpose.

(vii)

Layer by layer
The basket rises
Worked in
And pivoted
With bodkin and tallow
The neatness secured
Nature's design
Making ends meet
A wooden board
For a backrest
Cold floor
Lapping at their heels
The art of sitting
In a damp shed
Harnessed for life
The withy beds
Work horse
Of the Wetlands
The slender orchestra
Weaving beneath the sky
Swaying in the breeze
Every foot
A slug of willow
Slick dab of the wrist.

Dave Boobyer, Stathe

Rose knots

Gadsby's Boiler, Stathe

Withy Web, Hector's Yard

Serena's Geese

Withy Man

Snipe Shooting, Midelney, St Andrew's Day

Odd Glimpses - Henley, Othery, Burrow Bridge & Stathe

Mud, geese and barbed wire,
Teal and withies,
Flapping in the wind - black plastic.

Curlew and crack willow,
Digger and lapwing,
Swan and skylark - strange bedfellows.

Huddled beside the wall,
Clustered cottages -
Safe anchorage beneath the mump.

Settlers and pioneers,
Each plot of land staked out -
Like a claim in the goldrush.

Shovels, sandbags and boats,
A careful eye on the wind -
Each tide walking the plank.

Droves and dark ditches,
Newly dug, long lines of spoil,
Half eaten by sky - ricks.

Sowy River, Lang Acre Rhyne,
Sleek water in tandem -
Elegant ambassadors.

Chimneys and old cars,
Wriggly tin, chickens and sawbenches -
Independent orchards.

Saved and shored up, pumped out,
Shacks without foundations -
Enclosure, a family affair.

Dog, waders, balaclava,
Emergency rations -
Shotgun cartridges.

Oath Lock   Burrow Mump

Here the tide stops	The round tump
Or not as the case may be	A lump, below which
Canute would be proud	Delved in mud
Of the green gates	Three rivers joined
The simple mechanism	A tryst held firm
Winding down	Safety to spy upon
The power to stop	The tidal reach
And start the river	The tax both ways
In one man's arms	Overstepping
The regulation	Ancient walls
Of the water flow	The Gert Dog of Langport
The juddering force	Its wet nose
The long gallery	Nuzzled into a drain
Of river flotsam	Manipulating
Rising and falling	Dark water
Here where the withy beds	Each level, a toll
Still rattle	A history of effort
Boilers smoke	The crossing place
The salt edged tide.	Sacrifice, redirected.

Stanmoor to Curload

Here the houses
Lean, tumble
Gawk up at the sky
Cling to the bank
Back to the river
No surrender
A defiance
A resilience
Defended
To the last
Sandbag
The right to live
A passing trade
To fish and dip
A strange feeling
When the bank
Is about
To give
And the water
Sucking
All
Before it.

Stoke to Curry

Hovering
Between
West Sedge
And
Stanmoor
Withy yards
And
Baskets
Wedged
The smell
Of tannin
Cider
The road
To Helland.

Athelney

Nothing drastic
Just a place
To live
Safe
Amidst
The swamps
Native cunning
At its best
The force
Outwitted
Anglo-Saxon
Guerrilla
Tactics.

Aller Court

Here he brought them
And with water calmed them down
They stayed, in a manner of speaking.

Westonzoyland Pumping Station

Slender, above the never ending
Flatness, the chimney
Raises its own steam
A peculiar corner of history
Stoked up periodically
The boiler of enthusiasm
Pumping vitality
Into sluggish water
Seductive, the piston's motion
Sliding effortlessly
Along well worn lines
The graceful arc
Rhythmically fulfilled
Precision pinioned on a calliper
The engineer's eye
Artful and cunning
Ideas pulsing behind red brick
A temple of ingenuity
Battling with levels
Subservient acres
Drained and dissected
By countless ditches
Acts of Parliament
Regurgitated into the Parrett.

Digger

Lonely, perched
Precariously
On the bank's
Edge
Praying mantis
Looking
For a mate
Deftly
Swipes
The dark
Oozing
Sludge
Reaches out
Far
Into the river
Teeth
Sink in
And the bucket
Scrapes
Salt and sewage
Chains rattle
A warning cry
Or is it
Something else?

Living on the Edge

Carroll Gray's Milking Bail, Saltmoor

Keith Elvering

Elver Men on The Parrett

Dusk on the rising tide   lanterns and thermoses filled
Men and boys   prime themselves
In various watering holes   Thatchers Arms, King Alfred
Black Smock, trudge around   looking macho
In heavy boots   boilersuits and white socks
Like submariners   plot tides and times
Log each batch   willing each vulnerable convoy
Within their grasp   in huddled whispers
Sift information   try to predict
The unpredictable   moon's pattern
Elver psychology   and when all is decided
Talk long and loud   order more drinks
Thumph each other on the back   before desporting themselves
On the river bank   a clan of nightwatchmen
Poachers   fathers and sons
Best mates   in-laws and outlaws
Gangsters   each patch
A small ledge staked   earmarked
Carved out with a pick helve   jealously guarded
The right to hunt   stand and gather
Each year   hitting the same spot
The same primitive urge   irresistible call
River's pull   tribal activity.

Elver Dealing in Bridgwater, 2 am

The dealer sits on a stool	orange glow parked up
Like late night Fish and Chips	hooker with an army jacket
Knees covered	draws the customers out
Unmarked vans	one by one
Sail by	scruffy with long poles
Strapped to roof-racks	laden with nets
White gauze, curved wings	moths to a lamp
Their cargo, pale gelatinous	wriggling trays of currency
Weaving from the Sargasso	ambassadors, Atlantic ooze
Hoicked from the river's darkness	journey's end
Inspected with torches	thin filaments weighed
Threading the night's wages	addictive, like cocaine
With infinite precision	the barter banter
Croupier-paymaster-banker	deals his cards
Promises which do the rounds	backstreets, sorted
A fist full of fivers	fair exchange
Knock on the van door	unshaven, glint of earrings
A kilo or two	synchronised swimming
In the keep tank	counter-intelligence
Re-stocking rumours	gourmets and polders
Chinese Takeaways	chinese whispers
Threats in triplicate	cash in suitcases
Elvers hijacked	sleek sorcery
Far Eastover, one way package	sliding inland
Taoist delicacy	aphrodisiac.

'a wriggling tray of currency'

Eel Characteristics

Eel-slippy slimey slither
Twist, jive, jerk and thrust
Flick, knit and knot
Writhe and wriggle
Curves coil and convulse
Form and re-form
Thrash and spasm
Elegant in a strange
Kind of way
Sleek and speedy
Length and breadth
One long muscle
A torpedo
Living in the fast lane
Of slow flowing rivers
Perfectly formed
For that kind of thing
Lurking, in dark dank ditches
Not easily conned
Murky mud, their occupation
Will swallow anything
Rayballing, their undoing
Fyke nets, ancient traps
On the silver run

Seven long years
they wait
till the moon is dark
waters filling
wind
in the east
only then
will they slide
silvery
over meadows
hunt the sea
are gobbled up
by the ocean
search
the water
return radar
switched on
the homing device
holiday for two
in the Caribbean
last mystery
unsolved,
perplexing
even for scientists

Streamlined jaws
sharp and deadly
punish unwary flesh
picked up with gloved hands
thrust into hessian sacks
driven off at high speed
wet rendezvous with a smoker
meet their end in a deep freeze
slow cooling of arctic waters
better than a blow to the head
or a tub of salt
the knot disentangled
gutted, strung up
like quivers of fletched arrows
nodding monks
they meet the oak smoke
as if swimming again
firm and succulent
flesh, dark delicacy
retrieved from the swamp
vacuum packed
and sent abroad
their last wish fulfilled
migrating at last.

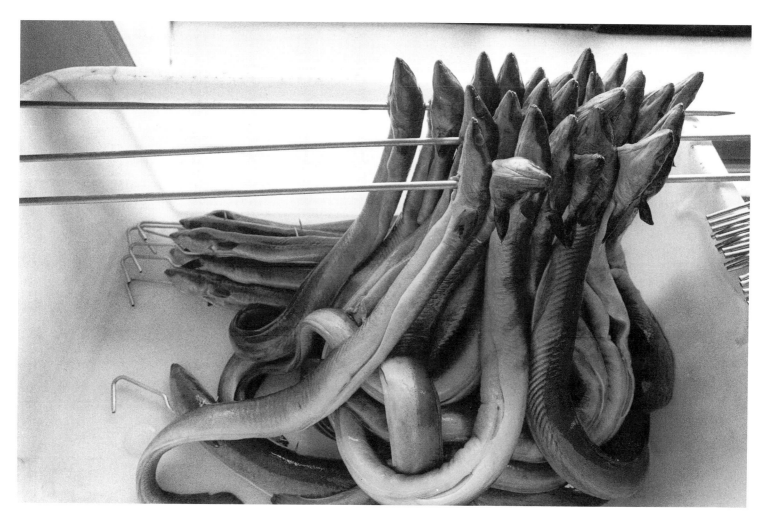

Spiked

Michael Brown, Eel Smoker

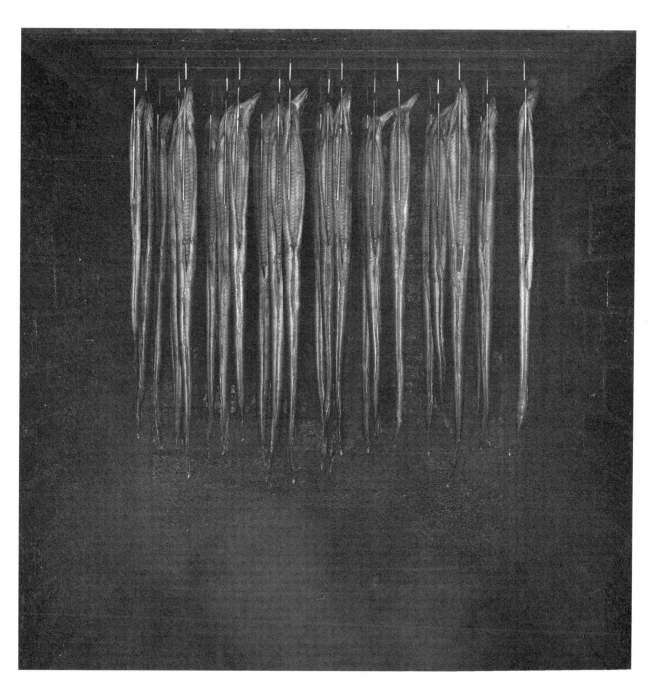

'Dark Delicacy'

After Sedgemoor

Locked in church	their minds' sacrifice
Spinning uneven odds	reeling, after night attack
Dabbling in politics	till the powder ran out
The call of Monmouth	full moon and a thick mist
Scythes against cannon	'Gaffer Scott's Vagabonds'
Flushed out like wildfowl	cut down in the corn, by the King's Horse
Langmoor Rhine	Bussex and the Plungeons
Kirke's Lambs and Trelawney's	mopping up before breakfast
Hung, drawn, entrails burnt	chains, the smell of hot tar
Beheaded, quartered	boiled in brine, preserved like meat
Displayed on poles	for several years. The Video Nasty
"Rebellion in your Home Town"	shades of Hieronymous Bosch
Or else sold into slavery	unexplained absence from the parish
Five shillings a denouncement	the price of a man's life
"Don't waste ye court's time"	"Ten years in Barbados"
Somerset transplanted	the rebellious spirit fed to sharks
En route, sold to plantations	fifteen pounds a man. No escape
The futures market	'FT' branded on the forehead
'Fugitive Traitor'	the Financial Times, indelibly printed
Caribbean Index	alphabet on the brow.

The Upper Crust

Turned King's evidence	bought pardons, a brisk trade
Edmund Prideaux of Forde Abbey	£14,760
Lady Churchill had wanted him	Azariah Pinney only £65
His own passage to the Caribbean	the screaming skull of Bettiscombe
Stored in a cardboard box	a reminder of the Judge
Kidney stones on the bench	alleviated by copious draughts
Weak punch	the acid remark
Painful urination	not lost on his victims
Surgery, undergone by Pepys	did not appeal
Dame Alice Lisle	aged 80, widow in Winchester
Condemned to be burnt alive	two dissidents
Unwittingly harboured	one a minister
Her last and only wish	to be beheaded cleanly. Granted
Hannah Hewling of Lyme	pleaded with the Judge not to quarter
Her brother, William	she clung onto the carriage wheel
Offered £100 for two days reprieve	her other brother, Benjamin in Taunton
Would cost a thousand	a simple burial in one piece
She was whipped	He ate sturgeon.

Monmouth Himself

Amy Farrant pointed / they found him, under an ash
Exhausted, unshaven / speechless and trembling
Bracken and shepherd's clothing / no disguise in a ditch
In his pockets / a few note books
Charms, prayers, songs / a handful of peas, a few guineas
The Order of the Garter / but no snuff box

He was safe whilst still afloat / in the rowing boat, beyond the Cobb
But the moment he smelt seaweed / the idea became a reality
The undercliff beckoned him / large rounded pebbles
A warning for his unsure feet / all would not be well
The long walk to the scaffold / the Crown, a glittering illusion
Lingered just long enough / time for Jack Ketch to find his axe
But not long enough to sharpen it / five blows and a lesson from Uncle James
Treason, legitimacy, rebellion / Catholicism and scrofula

Three children, an estranged wife / he left behind
A split family / dysfunctional at best
How he must have longed for / the smell of seaweed
The chance to turn back... / the beguiling warmth
The charms of Henrietta / Lady Wentworth.

Two Somerset Girls

Her lover condemned she chose the only course
In the aftermath of battle open to her beauty
No name or age or village the Colonel
She pleaded for his life seeing he was onto a good thing
Played with her conscience laid forth a proposition
Any sane person would in the circumstances
Think hard upon it offered herself, fair maid
Game, as she then was before marriage
Intact and virtuous and yet not so discreet
Her lover's life hanging by a thread
She took the bait the hours of darkness
We can only surmise more to his liking than hers
He pulled the curtains aside roughly at dawn
Showed her his precious handiwork in the courtyard
Dangling, her lover's body still twitching

The second girl, Mary Bridges aged 11, of Westonzoyland
Employed another technique altogether sharper
The ladies of her mother's house insulted
In fear of their honour simply drew the man's sword
And without a second thought stabbed him through the heart
Colonel Kirke not one to be squeamish
Courtmartialled her upon the evidence
Acquitted her honourably gave her back the sword
A reminder of Somerset ways young girls, and the cutting remark.

Bridgwater

Bricks and tiles	the legacy of clay
Fingered and fired	scooped out of the earth
All shades	red and ochre
Mingled in	with slime batches and schooners
Ketches and cottages	bath bricks
Trows and flatners	skippers and pilots
Fish and coal	timber and cattle cake
Sand, gravel	tramp steamers and hobblers
Parrett Barges	shirts and bandoliers
Cellophane	black plastic bags
Glass kilns and lead	squibs and bores
Carnivals	carnivores
History in the making	Christabella's breast
For Cromwell and Fairfax	bared on the rampart
Nonplussed by the pot shot	a royalist taunt
From the city walls	the wet nurse besieged
Breached to a cinder	Lady Wyndham undone
Hot stuff	Parliament's revenge.

West Street, Bridgwater

Albert Street Cutting

Sky and sky water   the ripple reflected

Navvies worked here   remember that
The smell of sweat   and horsedrawn barges

Heaving at the bow   the rope's tension
Full and powerful   hovering in the distance

The echo of heavy hooves   a taut sinew

The tow path   tugging at the water
Under bridges quivering   shadow of shadows

Between   these baulks of timber
Braced and bolstered   a narrow cleft
A cleavage   a corridor of light and dark

Coal, clay and limestone   tiles and bricks
Grain and timber   cider, sheep and cattle
These passed here   without a word

Keep the silence   take it home
A silver thread   to line your pocket.

'a corridor of light and dark'

Overheard in a Bridgwater Kitchen Late One Night
When the teenage son comes back out of his head, c. early 1970's

If 'eel do this 'eel do anything, "Trouble over Bridgwater"
I ask you, that Elvers Presley got a lot to answer for
"Cider and Garthunkel", "Rock around the clock", Steart to Huish
If only the world knew. Mark my words, Brent Knoll, Tone it down a bit
Isle got an Inkley Yeo'll find out one day. Beauchamp powders run out...
T'will all Combwich to us in the end. Chard and Crewkerne
Burnham on, Burnham on, Burnham on Sea... Ilminster at last
Don't piddle on the Parrett, H'eel knows no fury like an elver scorned

Moorland of this and I'll Burrow Bridge you, Othery you'll be
On your Cannington, Stretcholt and Stolford, Hamp that Dimmer
You can't take the Pathe, Aller all this you'll have to take the Oath
Puriton or not, Dunball and Chedzoy, Dunwear and Parchey, Evercreech
That'll be better for you Middlezoy, No more Kingsbury
And don't ELI to me, You're a Thorney in my side
Helland high water, Huntspill and Burtle, Meare Green again
Don't Shapwick me, Drayton narrow, that's what you want
Not too Muchelney, Midelney road for you, Henley come here
Nythe and fork, Stoke that Curry Gregory, or I'll Stathe you
It's Curload over the top already, Rivel this and Rivel that
Enmore and I'll Mallet you, Swell your Wick, Pitney
And that'll be your Langport... Sowy come here.

The Explosives Factory

There's nothing there on the two and a half inch map
But there are clues silence
A small curved branch line stops dead in a wet field
The perimeter fence snares ditches
Even the odd drove High Security
Measured out hidden parameters
Puriton non-conformist
Old pumping station glit of blue
Red brick kingfishers' nest
Smoke and steam between poplars
Chimneys of a chemical nature
A black hole stockpiled trapeze act
Double bluff vortex
Sucking men and women in lips hermetically sealed
Stirred not shaken Ordnance surveyed
The Official Secret red in the black ditch
Ducks with no feet on a certain tide
Eyes and throat smart followed by a black car
Elvering and like all black cars
In the early hours keeps its distance
The acid test in the mirror
Which was never there which was never there.

Spuddling around Burtle: Shapwick, Catcott and Ashcott

Swans and fen carr,   alder and birch
Hiss of rain   electricity lines
High voltage   sizzle like fried eggs
Low flying iets   zap the quiet world
Yellow diggers   parked up like toys
Dwarfed, black mountains   crumbling peat
Dredged up   from the squidgy mass
A vast sponge   upon which the road rests
Wobbles like jelly   articulated
The language of lorries   careers round corners
Places that can only just   keep head above water
At any moment   slip back without trace

Peat will suck a horse in   preserve a beetle
Suck a tractor in   preserve a trackway
Fuel a kiln   suck a man in
Skin and bone   the last meal
A wooden god   sacrifice
The astronomy   odds and ends
Artefacts   pots and sherds
Amber, jet   shale and antler
Loom weights, beads   Celtic beans, woad
Fat hen, spelt and emmer   seeds from long ago
That have gone the distance   a half life of their own.

Ancient Trackways

Crossing
And re-crossing
Soft Marsh
That preserved
Their memory
Damp
Like Furniture
Left out
In the rain
Too long
Wooden planks
Pegged
And protruding
A lattice
Above the water
Villages
That once stood
On stilts
Whose feet
Pulsed along
These boards?
Who was chasing who?
Woodsmoke, spears
Dried blood
On the sword.

Peat Cutting

Deftly   they take the first awkward cut
the next is better
The peat   darker, deeper till it glistens black
black with centuries
Black   like stout, a sheen like velvet
the wall of cotton-grass
Sedge   reed and reedmace
iris and sphagnum moss
Timesgrasp   decomposing in the darkness
in the wetness
Imperceptibly   layer by layer
year by year
Blocks   cut and cut again
raised and pivoted
Slid out   like dark loaves
mumps from a vast oven
Chopped   and then split down into turves
dried in lines, windrows
Shadowy walls   balanced precariously
each hyle self contained
Each ruckle   a monument, unshackled
brought to the door
Each turf   dark harvest
slowly perfecting itself
Hard, brittle   breaks with a crack. Winter's warmth.

117

Water Hanging

Water hanging
Lying low in pockets
Spuddling around
Man's endeavours
To divert and contain
A pockmarked mirror
Land half-reflected
Through pollarded withies
As if a vast waterhole
Was drying up
A tidal flood receding
Old friend
Departing into
The underworld
Sucked back
A feeling
Of wonder and loss
As if quicksilver
Was already
Slipping
Through
Your fingers.

Stogursey Castle

An island round
Floats in its own reflection
A ring of moat-water
Bright-laden with mallard and teal
Cruise, then scuttle
Beneath the drawbidge
Slender arches, avenues of light
The flight pond, slight weir
Crumbling walls, an oasis
From the modern world
Surrounded by grazing sheep
Heads down and nonchalant
The thatched gate house
Still inhabited
Winks its one long-bow slit
The shaft of past uncertainty
An arrow in time
Whistling
Through the clean air
Sharpened to a fine point
Encircled, a fish rises
A ring within a ring.

Stogursey Castle

Combwich

The Estuary - One Tide
From Combwich to Steart via Fenning Island

Salmon pink, just turned   the great metallic sheen
Cold sky, brittle, taut   pulling at the cold water
The flow accelerating   regurgitated eddies
Slow and yet strong   like the Ganges or the Brahmaputra
An unwinding, a letting go   the shedding of a skin

Tethered like goats, at odd angles   small boats lie stranded, wet grass
Waiting for the next sudden surge   empty and yawning, the filling basin
The pill an amphitheatre   sleek, steep, sleeping, slithering
River mud, thick grey skin   shines like the hide of a hippopotamus
The foreshore anchored   riven by gaudy rivulets
Small gullies ebbing   seek the fallen tide
On whose rim oystercatchers   feed and preen, pipe, trill and whistle
Like sailors dance the hornpipe   and just as evasive, fly off
A black and white strobe   shimmering in a haze of wingbeats

Circle, dart, jive and tack   skew and slew, skive and flock
Settle again. Orange-red beaks   stab the mud, prise apart their booty
Seek the succulent mussel   ragworm, lugworm and cockle
True connoisseurs, maritime diet   healthy and abundant, a vast menu
Stretching around the last bend   island of sound treacherous to shipping

Fickle channel, navigation flawed last resting place of ketches and trows

Hulks slewed, the fatal grounding submerged graveyard

Skeletons lie, lean ghosts ribs picked clean, punctuate the mud

Grovel in the river bed Davy Jones and Davy Jones

Wait for the next tide and slide ever more deeply into the locker

The grey-brown shifting mirror that stretches further and further

Towards the flat nub of a coast that is only a low wall

A few stubborn farmhouses shelter with their backs to the wind

And the west channel squalls of sordid rain

Plunder the sky, steal the light sleek horizon of never ending mud

Mercantile and seagoing thin slices of shingle, storm fed

Lurk behind reed beds weave and wave, rustle their plumage

Rich ripple on the shoreline shared with sheep, scrawny and scraggy

Graze salt-goose marsh beneath the hum of electric cables

Beachcombers, bleak and coastal the lurking presence outwitted

Outmanoeuvred by wildfowl and waders

Ripe pickings in winter long shadow housed on the horizon

Cracking legacy a feeling of unease, uncertainty

Estuary, end of river sudden waves spew and spray

Manic, the shriek and screech raw, untamed channel

Unleashed, unfettered freedom calling sharply

Transient and tumultuous pierces the salt wind

Sea meadow caught and snared Tide pounces.

Steart

Tacky Shades

Hinkley 'A'

Hinkley Point: The Guided Tour

First the video / driven off to the 'other world'
Then the white helmets with liners / squashed into the back
Then the ear plugs / of a cramped minibus
Shaped like violets / like fuel rods
Just in case we should get / ushered in by electronic gates
A whiff of the truth / the bored gaze of a policeman

The list of names is handed over / the vehicle number plate
School children and pensioners / no doubt already clocked and checked
We stand out like sore thumbs / on the way in I had waved cheekily
Laden with cameras and awkward questions / to the security cameras. Not a wise move

The first thing to report / the second thing to report
A man asleep, sunning himself / the noise of the turbine hall
Behind a shed, near the nursery / the worried looks of the workers
Where they produce the scant flowers / 'routine' maintenance
That pepper the plant / with one reactor already shut down

Our guide, Sheila, a motherly figure / Yes they do pump in
Given the job of handling 'casuals' / a million gallons of seawater a minute
As we are called, and far from casual / 74 tons a second
She regurgitates facts and figures / a cat has nine lives
And proves beyond all reasonable doubt / a nuclear reactor has only one
That it is all very, very safe / but who inspects the mousetrap?

Hinkley 'B'

Brendan Sellick

Mud-Horseman

A small figure	getting smaller
With a basket	over his shoulder
Shoreline	studded with beacons
Houses receding	backs turned

Low crust	sea wall
Extends the sky	glistens
Sucking mud	pulling him outwards
Towards the wind	singing in the nets

Long lines of poles	laden with silver
The nets cargo	dangling, trapped
Still flapping	eyes and gills
Eels and flatfish	skate and prawns

Shrimps and mullet	Dover sole
Sea bass and salmon	odd nips
Seal and conger	Flatholm and Steepholm
The long trudge back	uphill grind, sea defences

The weight	begins to tell
The tipping out	sorted, washing in the shed
Deep freeze	the long shadow
Getting longer	sledge put away.

Skate and Shrimps

The Last Man

Notes

Naming the Parrett: This is not a John Cleese sketch though it could easily have been one. There are more than enough dead Parretts. The infomation is derived from a book called 'English River Names' by Eilert Ekwall published by OUP in 1928. The deductions are not entirely conclusive but then the Celtic world seen through Anglo Saxon eyes and ears never is. Another alternative 'long-shot' is the Cornish word 'pedrevanns' which means to crawl, which is exactly what elvers do when they come into the bank, once the tide has stopped pushing.

The Celtic Mirror: There are only a handful of these in existence. They are usually found associated with a burial; in this case that of a woman. This particular mirror was found in 1995 on a farm where I go sheep shearing at Portesham, south of Dorchester. The design is, for me at least, extraordinarily powerful and I use it here at the beginning of the book as an analogy for the hidden unknown past that lurks beneath our landscape, and in Celtic terms the 'Other world'. Today we have all but forgotten the spiritual world of our ancestors. The drawing is by the farmer's daughter Chloe Fraser. This mirror, which is in design somewhere between the Desborough and Birdlip mirrors, is now held by the Dorchester Museum. A similar one was found at Holcombe, near Uplyme, a few years ago. My own feeling about these wonderful designs is that they have certain similarities in spirit with the world of Scythian Art. Nobody knows their exact function; they could just as easily be shamanic masks. The Iron Age tribe that lived here then was called the Durotriges, who lived not only where Dorset is today but interestingly enough controlled a wedge-shaped corridor of land that included the length and breadth of the Parrett... with the Dobunni to the north and the Dumnonii to the west. They had access from the English Channel to the Bristol Channel and would have been a corridor for trade with Wales and Ireland. This mirror dates from about 55AD.

The Source: There are, as the poem implies, many sources to the River Parrett and I have not taken an obvious one, though one or two do exist. Namely the ponds in the grounds of that rather wonderfully eccentric hotel, Chedington Court. I have kept the source simple and anonymous as it would have been three thousand years ago. A place in all probability of Celtic spring worship, as there is a church nearby. The Celts believed that the sources of rivers and streams were an eye into the 'Otherworld', and many of these sites later became early Christian places of worship, and as such are still held in high regard in parts of West Cornwall. The whole area abounds in trickles, springs and oozes. Just behind the long beech ridge lies the source of another river, the river Axe, which flows to the English Channel. Other springs to the north east flow into the Yeo system and Sutton Bingham reservoir. Eventually of course these join the Parrett.

Early Stages: South Perrott is the first village. It is the point at which the first clutch of streams come together. The history of this part of Dorset and Somerset is so interlinked with flax and hemp, rope and sail making, that the analogy of the streams forming a ship's hawser is entirely appropriate. South Perrott is also the first crossing place, though drivers rarely notice it, unless the road is under water. It seems strange that there should be two streams here. The water going downhill and the traffic going uphill. Millers terms abound but the word grist, interestingly enough, refers not only to corn about to be ground, the action of grinding and corn that has been ground, but the size and thickness of yarn or rope.

Ham Hill: From here you see it all... An aerial view of mid-Somerset and a place no doubt of great strategic importance in the past. If you squint you can see source and mouth, and if you look even more closely you realise the complexity of land tenure, enclosures, history, rebellions etc. It's all there. A marvellous spot, and one used, not infrequently, in the early hours. I used to do night lambing at Batemore and every year would park my caravan on top, behind a barn overlooking Montacute. The farm hand Ted, who came from the Levels, assured me he had found elvers in the ditches at the bottom of the hill.

The history of Ham Hill and the villages surrounding it is very rich in anecdote. It was the site of many contentious meetings including one by Joseph Arch, an outspoken leader of the farm workers in the last century seeking fair wages and conditions of work. Not long after this there was a gathering of about five thousand people in a tented camp who waited for the end of the world, in fulfilment of one of Mother Shipton's prophecies. This devout yet gullible congregation believed they alone would survive the imminent Flood, and apparently in between devotions cavorted around naked and engaged in certain procreative activities. Only on the third day did they realise, when the mist cleared, that the world as they knew it had not disappeared. And rather sheepishly followed their minister back down the hill. This was in the late 1870's, and may well have been the precursor of the Glastonbury Festival.

Ham Hill Stone: This stone is wonderful in colour and has been quarried for hundreds of years. Some villages are almost entirely made out of it, even East Coker, though Eliot refers to the 'grey' stone. Geologically Ham Hill stone is a shelly limestone and this covers the less resistant Yeovil sands which outcrop on the lanes leading down off Ham Hill and indeed many of the lanes around Yeovil as well. These are sunken and produce the most extraordinary shapes and folds, with bare tree roots growing out of the clefts and crevices in a most dramatic way. The stone is still worked by Ray Harvey and a team of twelve workers.

Ramblings - Sluice & Weir: In the upper reaches of the Parrett the water levels are controlled by several weirs and sluices, and these play a major part, not only in flood relief, but in maintaining water levels during the summer. Sheep and cattle rely on this to keep the grazing up together. The other main reason, apart from preserving the many different habitats that live in and around rivers, is to provide power for the old mill systems which abound in these upper reaches of the Parrett.

What interests me is the clear division of water behaviour above and below each weir. Haselbury Mill, Bow Mill, Carey's Mill, Gawbridge Mill and Thorney Mill are the most obvious, with other mills on tributaries, like Haymore Mill, Tail Mill and Lopen Mill. The latter was the site of the Flax and Linen Research Institute which was set up during the Second World War.

The weir described is actually the one at the Parrett Works. The grove of bat willow opposite has just been cut down but, I am glad to see, replanted. For a fully comprehensive book on river and pond life see 'The Natural History of the Somerset Levels' by Bernard Storer, a goldmine of information.

The Parrett Works: An ancient and interesting site which became a centre for an iron works and other industrial ventures. George Parsons took it over in 1854, moving from Lower Farm, West Lambrook. The wheel was installed and built to a design by William Fairbairn. It was here that George Parsons started his empire. Coal and pig iron was brought up from Long Load. Amongst his many machines were those used in the linen and rope making industry, as well as steam engines, threshing machines and general foundry work. They employed about 150 people and had a works band. Unfortunately the company ran into financial difficulties and was liquidated in 1870. In 1873 George Parsons emigrated to Kaikoura in New Zealand where he became involved with his three sons in the flax industry again. Maybe it is no coincidence that my brother, who lives in New Zealand, should have found an old waterwheel with 'Petherton' stamped on it. He hopes one day to resuscitate it for making paper.

The Parrett Works main building is owned by Nick Sloane who also runs the Parrett Press and is a skilled letter cutter doing a fair bit of work for Ian Hamilton Findlay. His present commission involves 38 tons of Portland stone bound for an olive grove in the south of France. The inscription is part of Michelet's 'L'histoire de la Révolution française'.

Burrow Hill Cider Farm: I include this poem for the sake of completeness. It first appeared in 'Blood Earth Medicine'. The floods that occur in Somerset are not just the variety you see near rivers, but can include apples, eels, elvers, even 'grockles'. The cider farm is well worth a visit in the autumn when the pressing is under way. The general public have almost forgotten what good cider should taste like, so conditioned are they to fizzy processed apple concentrate. Orchards are a great asset and some sheep shearers used to drive into a farm, test the cider, and if it wasn't any good drive on out again, without even looking at the sheep. Alas fewer and fewer farmers have the time and inclination to make their own cider and regard orchards as an incoefficience rather than as a necessity. White yuppy designer cider however is not good for sheep shearers, though the bottles can be used for drenching sheep in emergencies.

The Spirit Level: This is of course a reference to the Cider Brandy distillery at Thorney Halt which was once a milk factory and munitions store during the war. The railway which went from Yeovil to Langport linked the two London lines and went across the Moors. The production of cider brandy has been going on since 1987. I remember working both Josephine and Fifi during the flood which cut off Muchelney for two weeks. Both stills were made in Paris in the thirties by Gazagne. The art of distilling cider is one which goes back a very long way. I have in my possession some acts of parliament from George III's reign which state that cider for distilling should be exempt the normal cider tax, i.e. it would be taxed later under another fiendish scheme. These references last for 100 years at least, starting in Queen Anne's reign. So the distilling of cider must have been a recognised and lucrative source of revenue. The earliest reference is in Worlidge of 1678 (seven years before the Battle of Sedgemoor), referring to it as cider brandy. The recent hullabaloo with Brussels, the Spanish Government and the Scotch Whisky Association have only highlighted the general ignorance that surrounds this spirit.

The Spirit Bond: Cider making is a noisy rumbustuous affair; distilling is relatively quiet, stable and clean. The bond is totally silent, dark, and mysterious. Each barrel has its own history logged down. Past spirits that have been through it, the colour, age, volume, the evaporation, the angel's share. All these add to the spirit's history. Some barrels mature faster than others. Oak makes a mountain of difference and some coopers will choose their oak from a particular region. Old sherry casks are used, and their value is actually increased by being second hand. Other barrels used are Jack Daniels and Bourbon and white rum. All spirit is clear when it is made. The final analysis hinges on the bond and the skill in blending. The spirit is approx 70% proof when it comes off the still, and this has to be brought down carefully to 42%. Eau de Vie is now on tap.

Thorney Mill: Mentioned in Domesday this mill belonged to Muchelney Abbey and was worked until 1966. The wheel was made by Coombes of Beaminster in 1866 and can still be worked, the millstones and chutes are still in place. At present it is the home of Evelyn Body, a sculptor. The new computerised system of sluice gates was put in about seven years ago, replacing a man on a bicycle who used to shoot mink. On the other side of the sluice gate is a half lock which was used for getting barges further up the river towards Kingsbury and Gawbridge. The mill was owned by Bradfords who then moved their base to Crewkerne railway station.

Carp: They are really big and love sunbathing in the shallows. They do grow to a fair size, and in times of shortage they provided a useful bit of protein.

Kingfisher: They do fly ever so fast, and like guided missiles home in. Then sit waiting for admirers, live off other things apart from fish.

Somerset Light: Self evident, except that we take internal light for granted now, electricity having been with us for quite a while. The windows in older houses, and even the houses themselves are situated to get the best advantage with light, and in several I have noticed the autumn equinox light hitting the fireplace. Whether this is design or coincidence is difficult to say, but re-kindling the hearth is an important event. Perhaps if farmers had driven their cattle through fire at Beltane there wouldn't have been all this trouble with BSE. The winter light on the moors and levels has its own characteristics, which after a while can be a little depressing if the fog lasts for a week. However, the clear light of winter which eventually emerges more than makes up for it. Sometimes there is only a thin band of mist at about 3 feet which means you can see the cows' legs but not their bodies. Many painters are drawn to Somerset light, which with floods is accentuated and reflected. Most of Somerset's light now comes from Hinkley.

Heron Fishing: Again self evident. The sheer quantity of herons in some parts of the moors is astounding. There are heronries at Swell Wood, Midelney and Somerton. When they have young, they fish in the open more and more. They have a kind of prehistoric feel to them, rather like the Ibis. Young herons look like punks and behave about the same. Once John Leach told me he found three herons looking in a dip in the grass with no more than an inch or two of water in it. Were they being vain or was it just worms?

Heron Rising: Only when a heron gets up do you realise that it's there. And the size of it. Eels yes, I have seen a cormorant take one, and these cormorants are getting more numerous and I hope that they do not compete adversely with the herons. They seem to have bully boy characteristics and hang out on electricity poles in gangs of 12 or 15.

John Leach's Woodkiln: This pottery in Muchelney is so well known that little comment is needed. The firing which occurs about every three weeks is a monumental labour, for the kiln requires stoking more or less continuously for 36 hours with offcuts, both soft and hard wood. The kiln temperature has to reach approx 1300°C which is high by any standards, and the kiln has two chambers. This is of course in the tradition of John's grandfather Bernard who worked in Japan with Hamada. A few years ago I stopped off in Japan on the way to New Zealand and met Hamada's son and we did a small pot exchange. The pottery in Mashiko is well worth a visit. At the end of the firing, Lizzie, John's wife, does a good spread for the workers. Cider and beer are welcome additions. The unloading follows a few days later when the kiln has cooled down sufficiently. The opening up is always a moment of excitement. With wood firing conditions are never quite the same, the all important glaze a tell-tale sign. When he first arrived John used to get peat from near Westhay to help fire his kiln. This was delivered by two brothers called Moss Bros. John Leach also has a coracle that he has kindly lent me on occasions to go on down the Parrett. In 1990 Muchelney was cut off for at least ten days and everyone had to be ferried around on tractors and trailers, even the school children.

In Time of Flood: A long poem and one which uses Anglo-Saxon alliteration, the strong half-line, the caesura. I make no apologies for it. When the river goes over the top there is no stopping it. You only have to look at the pictures of the floods in 1929 and the breach in the bank of the Tone at Athelney to realise the force which is contained behind those banks. It is alarming, at first, to realise that a fair bit of Somerset lives below river level and sea level. Put a tide on it, and a wind, and a flood, and you have a delicate situation. The part of the Parrett described is between Thorney and Langport. The Isle joins at Midelney, the Yeo at Huish Bridge. A few days of heavy rain, and the land is sodden, the water runs off much faster. Indeed the speed of flooding has increased with urban building and farmers' improved drainage. One time it happened so suddenly, I saw farmers two years ago driving their cattle off the moor late at night. When the rain stops, the floods do not abate, indeed the level always rises after that. And once the land is flooded it stays that way more or less, for a month or two. Farmers get £417 per hectare per year for this privilege and a fair bit of wildfowl shooting thrown in. Curry Moor has suffered badly in the last few years and there are various schemes afoot including a proper tidal barrage at Dunball. The Brue, the Huntspill, K.S.D. and the Axe all have tidal gates or clyses, but the Parrett is much larger and such a device would have to be carefully designed to prevent flooding in Bridgwater.

Wildfowl on West Moor: When I work at the cider farm at Burrow Hill I sometimes walk up the hill if I am early and look out over the flooding. As it goes down, various small bits of land re-appear, and I realised one day that a path existed across the water along the main drain. A small thread of land had just re-emerged. 'Flood walking', which at times meant going in well above the knee, was well rewarded. The number of wildfowl sheltering behind an old withy bed by Pitt Bridge was prodigious. The noise and sight was more akin to East Africa than South Somerset. The taking out of withy beds wholesale is I think wrong and anyone who has experienced a strong north east wind on the moors knows how much protection a withy bed can give. West moor was one of the last to be enclosed and drained in 1833. At the same time the Parrett Navigation Company was formed and the canal to Westport created. This was at the same time as the construction of the Chard Canal which went via Ilminster; another grand vision to link the Bristol Channel with the English Channel. A short cut to avoid going round Land's End and Cape Cornwall. Alas the railway came ten years later and scuppered the idea. The bridge and a drove is named after the Pitt family, Pitt the Elder being rewarded with a farm at Curry Rivel, apparently for his opposition to the cider tax during the Dutch wars, which at 5/- a hogshead was steep. The farm is one I have worked on dipping sheep and has long colonnades in the classical style. Pitt commissioned Capability Brown to erect a monument to the eccentric Sir William Pynsent and this commands a marvellous view over West Sedgemoor. A cow climbed up the tower one day in 1946, and being large could not turn round. They had to slaughter it at the top. Most people refer to it as the 'Cider' monument.

Great care should be taken not to disturb wildfowl.

Winter Levels: Self evident. The long battle between the seasons and the historical battle between the commoners and those that wanted to drain their land for their profit. The wrangles over the drainage is superbly documented in 'The Draining of the Somerset Levels' by Michael Williams (CUP). The early wrangles being between Glastonbury and Wells. Fish weirs were a constant source of debate as they led to widespead flooding and impeded the flow of water. Various banks were built and some deliberately broken to save lands from flooding. Needless to say communities would patrol their banks just in case their neighbours were tempted. Shot guns have been fired on more than one occasion. Surveyors were always distrusted by the local community as they are today. And none more so than the various attempts to drain King's Sedgemoor which defeated even Vermuyden. It was an early case of privatisation and those that bought into the scheme benefited immediately. The local people basically had their best land stolen from them in the name of improvement. One particular surveyor, Richard Locke, who advocated drainage passionately, was 'stoned, bruised and beat by the mob till the blood has issue from his nose mouth and ears' and his effigy burnt by the owners of geese. Shades of West Sedgemoor in 1982 when effigies of conservationists were burnt by farmers outside the Black Smock. A curious reversal of feelings; only they had a Sherman tank as well. Another surveyor in 1775, William Fairchild, was threatened with his life and they went so far as to dig his grave. A crowd of a hundred or two gathered and a prize of a hogshead of cider offered to anyone who could catch him. Meddlers beware. The flood of 1929 is still within living memory. Another tidal surge was in 1981 and affected the estuary severely.

Muchelney Abbey: Rather like 'Somerset Light' this is a portrait of Muchelney in one of those very clear cold frosty mornings.

This was on the way to work at the cider farm at about 7.30am in early December just as it was getting light. When the moors are flooded and the floods are followed by a very sharp prolonged frost, the whole area is transformed with hoar frost and ice into an almost magical landscape. 'Smeech' is a dialect word more often found in Dorset. It means puff of smoke or dust. 'Swallet' is a word borrowed from the Mendips, where it refers usually to an unexpected hole in the ground usually caused by a stream, either past or present. It can also refer to a hole caused by subsidence. 'Smeech' and 'swallet' have a peculiarly satisfying sound on the tongue. Swallets have been known to open up and take cows.

Another Early Morning: Just before the dissolution of the monasteries. A fair bit of building work did go on and the monks of Muchelney were well known for their freedom, private quarters and consumption of eels. They were reprimanded for their behaviour several times. It is the site of an earlier Saxon house that was destroyed by the Danes and later rebuilt by Athelstan. No doubt these same monks also started the process of draining the moors and containing the river. 'A place of isolation all right'. We can only wonder at what manuscripts and works of art must have been destroyed over the years. This poem first appeared in 'Secrets of the Levels' by Chris Chapman.

The Priest's House: A wonderful example of mediaeval architecture, and now in the hands of the National Trust. Twice the church tried to pull it down. It was saved in 1901 by the Society for the Protection of Ancient Buildings. A public subscription paid for its restoration. The donors included Thomas Hardy, Bernard Shaw and Jane Morris, the widow of William Morris. It has recently been restored again by English Heritage, and is lived in by Sir Anthony and Catherine Denny.

Fishermen on West Sedgemoor: Licences are granted for two rods per person. Some have six... Pollution (like the incident at Somerton in August 1995 where mercury and lindane were deliberately poured into a drain that fed a small stream leading to the Cary) does not help fish stocks. Silage effluent and mink take their toll. The eel population should perhaps be monitored more carefully. Usually fishermen complain about eels taking their bait, hook line and sinker. Not so often now. Otters are meant to be making a comeback and I have seen them and their tracks. They need cover and the clear fell policy adopted on certain parts of the Wetlands to prevent birds of prey does not encourage them.

The Priest Himself: The arrangements were as described. The advent of the Black Death, which 'came ashore' near Weymouth in October 1348, must have caused great panic, pestilence and soul searching, to say nothing of a shortage of labour and consequently food. No doubt it was the basis of many sermons, proper living, morals etc. In May 1349, the abbot died of the Black Death and a month later his successor went the same way. Above Melplash, Dorset, there is still a 'posie' tree.

Midelney: The home of the Trevilian family. This island is a law unto itself. Poachers will be 'hung drawn and quartered'. 'Land mines' are now in place I believe. This property was acquired by the family after the dissolution of Muchelney Abbey, and they have hung onto it ever since. Snipe shooting and hawking are the order of the day. In winter often the only way out is by tractor or four wheel drive. Midelney Manor is open on Thursday afternoons. The falcons' mews is now the kitchen.

The Underkeeper: Employed by John Trevilian, 'Mr. Buzzard' keeps four hawks. He has had several narrow escapes, the latest being in a car which he somehow managed to put into five foot of flood water late one night. He now rides a bicycle and is looking to buy a horse to go with his cart. He runs a spaniel with his hawks, and sometimes his ferrets. He wants to experiment with cormorant fishing as it was once done on the moors. He also works at the cider farm.

The Coracle: These have been made since neolithic times and are still made today, though not in Somerset. They are still in use on the Severn and the Wye and the Tywi for salmon netting. I have borrowed one from John Leach made by Peter Faulkener of Leintwardine, and very excellent it is to go off down the Parrett in flood. Getting in and out with steep slippery banks is however very awkward and at times dangerous.

The Old Canoe: Several have been dug up wonderfully preserved in the peat. This one is in the museum in Glastonbury and these artefacts give us an idea of the way of life when wetlands meant wetlands. The wetlands today should really be called drained lands, though there are moves to keep higher water level agreements in certain areas.

At Midelney Pumping Station: Built in the sixties this is one of the more modern pumping systems. Most of the others were built in the forties and are red brick. This is a bit of a monstrosity but it does the job. Where it is situated is one of the most interesting points on the whole water system, because not only do the two rivers, the Isle and the Parrett, join here, but the water is at all sorts of other levels. There was once a lock and a lockkeepers cottage here, and all barges going up to Westport would have to go through the system. Then there is the level of the main drain, the catchwater drain and on the other side Southmoor main drain. A complexity that takes some getting used to.

Shearing at Greinton: This was one of the hottest days I can remember shearing on the Levels. Not a breath of wind moved. Most Kiwi shearers shear in sheds so the novelty of shearing outside is a bonus. The only problem is not only do you lose vast quantities of sweat but the back of your neck is always exposed to the sun. I have heard of shearers getting kidney stones and nearly dying from heat exhaustion. Shearers can also be killed by bad electrics. It happened on Exmoor two or three years ago. As it happens, I have sheared not only at the source of the Parrett at Chedington, but at the mouth near Pawlett, and a fair few places in between. Kingsbury, Thorney, Muchelney, Wick, Curry Rivel, Henley, Moorland, to name a few.

Moor Names: Any more let me know.

End of an Era: Self explanatory. I always like to see the withies laid out in lines beside the river. Now no more.

Langport, c. 935AD: There is so much history here that it is difficult to know where to begin. Its importance as a port is well known, but its importance as a Royal Mint is less well known. The mint was for silver coins and was administered under the decrees of Athelstan 925-940. Fiddling the mint was not advisable. It is interesting to note that Stuckeys Bank produced the first banknotes on vellum and other advances in what we would call financial planning. East Indiamen were owned by Langport families and the barge traffic must have been quite a sight. Horses coming up to Bow bridge were galloped and then the lines cast as the barges shot through the bridge. Traffic had the choice of being unloaded at Gawbridge, Long Load or Westport. I used to work with Ray Stuckey on cider, though his economics were on a different scale from his ancestors.

Battle of Langport, 1645: There has been some dispute as to the actual site of the battle, but recent historians reckon it is on the site of the re-enactment which took place last summer on two very hot days. The retreating Royalist forces fired Bow Street and fled to Bridgwater.

The 'Gladstone': Evie Body showed me this battered account book a month or two ago and I simply abstracted some of the more interesting information. The Bank of Stuckey and Bagehot was well known in Langport and they owned a fleet of vessels of which the 'Gladstone' was just one. In bits of the ledger that have not been used, the miller of 1945-46 has made all his entries, showing family names that nearly all exist today.

A Rastafarian takes a walk from Langport to Monksleaze Clyce: Not all visitors are local and here I have tried to incorporate a city dweller's impression of the landscape, the railway line and the rubbish, as well as the rather extraordinary phenomenom of the Sowy river which takes water out of the Parrett and takes it to the

King's Sedgemoor Drain where it slowly regains the Parrett at Dunball. Some of this water is pumped back up onto Somerton moor. There is of course the old route of the Cary which was diverted a few times. The black stuff is of course peat which is still dug around Westhay, Burtle, Ashcott and Shapwick, etc. See 'Peat Cutting'. Read it as rap.

Withies: A long story, the rise and fall of a wetland industry. At one time there were several thousand acres of withy beds, a Victorian industry helped by two world wars. Not easy, the nurturing of a withy bed; disease, fungus, insect, frost, too much flooding at the wrong time, not enough weeding. A constant maintenance let alone the cutting by hand. A good man could cut forty bundles a day, an acre a week. A modern machine, two acres a day, and an acre could yield about 200 bundles. There is considerable skill in cutting and tying the withy bundles, with a rose knot. Quite a few of the small boilers and their tell-tale chimneys are still in use, but many look like they are on their last legs. The smell of boiling withy is not unpleasant, and one that carries over into the stripping shed. Slighty antiseptic, which it is; the basis of aspirin. The long lines of browns and buffs drying by the river are an unforgettable sight. Whites are obtained by steeping the rods and letting them grow on a bit before stripping them. The withy is so versatile that you can make anything with it, more or less; chairs, baskets, hampers, coffins, creels, dog baskets, tables, screens, hurdles, salmon pitchers, eel traps... each with their own variations to make the job in hand easier. Gas victims blinded in the First World War were often given basket-making as a therapeutic way of making a living. Various schemes have been devised to encourage withy growers to turn their land over to subsidy farming, favouring wildfowl above jobs. On West moor three out of four withy growers have recently given up, yet the demand for withies remains very high.

Odd Glimpses: These insights are no more than views or glimpses that you might catch out of the corner of your eye and yet that is the quality of the Levels and Moors. At every corner something new; an individual streak, a small holder's stubborn eccentricity, a sheepdog biting the tyres. Many of these places are of great historical interest. Some doubt has been thrown on Asser's account of Alfred, but his stand against the Danes is well known and the finding of the jewel at North Newton adds credence to his presence lingering in the Wetlands. After the battle of Ethandune Alfred is said to have converted the Danes, Guthrun and thirty warriors, and had them baptised as part of the surrender terms at Aller.

Westonzoyland Pumping Station: Unfortunately it doesn't pump any more but it was the first real attempt to use pumping and steam as a way of keeping the levels manageable. And this in 1830. It was not a great success. The pump was not man enough for the job and the cost to the local farmers was 5/- an acre. The original cost being £4000 and £250 a year to run it. The area affected being 1600 acres. Pumping alone would not cure the levels, but with more efficient engines it could help relieve the long term effects of flooding. Subsequently more and more red bricked small pumping stations appeared, culminating in the sixties architecture of glass, steel and electricity.

Digger: No longer do men slave away with shovels, up to their knees in slime. Various boats were devised to power-wash the banks but the next tide always brought it back. Weedcutters are still used on the Brue. Forks turned over make good rakes for weed. But the use of a digger or drag-line means the river is straightened and the bank itself built up at the same time. A fair bit of work has been done near Burrowbridge and on the Tone. Piling helps in certain places but sandbags are still visible. There is no easy answer. The slime batches did their bit in taking the silt off but they restricted the flow in flood as fish weirs did. A new device, a floating 'scourer', was tried in July 1996 and this appears to have been effective.

Eels, Elvers, Elver Men, Smokers and Dealers: Withies and cider are one thing, but elvers and eels are something else. A slippery business. Well within living memory elvers were plentiful. Bath loads of them were used for feed and fertiliser. But now delved out, their price varies like drug dealing. Whether they are in short supply because of vagaries of the Gulf Stream, Sargassso sea, pollution or overfishing, science has yet to inform us. The price varies normally between £30 and £60 per kilo but this year at the tail end of 1996 it reached £200. This is partly because of scarcities on the continent, but also because of far eastern interests who are prepared to pay high prices to supply eel farms in mainland China. No doubt the eels are sold onto Japan, but in effect they are encouraging over fishing and soon there will be no eels left, which is what has happened to the Japanese and Chinese eels. We are in effect selling the future for a pittance, a future stock that can never be replaced. Ireland perhaps has the right idea, by refusing to allow elvers to be sold outside its borders, encouraging long term natural re-stocking. Even the elver men and dealers realise that something must be done, either by having a close season or by restocking with a kilo per license. Maybe even these measures will not succeed. Some advocate a total ban, as with herring fishing a few years ago. Even now it maybe too late. The life cycle is about ten years; the elver being about three years old when it arrives and then waiting another seven before running to sea. It still has to get back to the Sargasso, and no firm proof has yet come forward that they even do return from here. Possibly it is only the American ones that return, and we get the elvers as a free gift due to the history of continental drift and the Gulf Stream. The change could be due to sunspots, global warming or even icebergs...

After Sedgemoor: The punitive nature of the reprisals seem barbaric today, but even the faintest whiff of treason was like nectar to a bee for wagging tongues. I do not think we can gauge in any way, except perhaps in Northern Ireland, the true divide that religion manufactured. And having a Catholic king brought with it a reversal of everything that the Protestants had fought for. The cause of individual freedom of religion and conscience. In a sense the Battle of Sedgemoor was a family squabble between James Scott Duke of Monmouth and his uncle James II, Charles II's Catholic brother. James II had no son, but two daughters, Mary and Anne. Mary was married to William of Orange. James Scott was born in 1649 to Lucy Barlow who had 'married' Charles in Liege when he was in exile. Lucy died at 27 when James was nine. Intrigues and plots were endemic. His political campaigning had more in common with the presidential hustings in America than normal court procedure. He even cured a woman called Elizabeth Parcet of scrofula in Hinton Park. The Duke's touch was seen by many as proof of legitimacy. The events leading up to Sedgemoor are well known but the fate of those that were transported is not so well documented. For a brilliant synopsis see 'The Monmouth Rebellion' by Robert Dunning who has written many other books on the history of Somerset. The Rebellion raises many issues and it is curious that Somerset should have been the scene of England's last major uprising, which still lurks in folk memory.

The Upper Crust: Money it seems could buy almost anything. The case of Alice Lisle was outrageous even at the time. But her husband had been one of the judges who had condemned Charles I to be beheaded. And Charles I was James II's father. The Hewling manuscript is still kept at the museum in Lyme Regis.

Monmouth Himself: He could have won. He was a good general, and had a large popular following. Bad luck and fate were against him, but he could have routed the Royalist forces. Numbers and surprise were on his side, but a disciplined well trained well armed and experienced force can often overcome a rabble, particularly if the rabble is unused to standing firm. Once caught, Monmouth didn't stand a chance. James II only lasted until 1688 when he fled in a rowing boat. William and Mary landed in Brixham. The standing Royalist army at that time having been increased to 30,000 not a lot different to today. Somerset has, hopefully, preserved a slightly independent free thinking rebellious streak. One of the many reasons that Monmouth lost was that two of his smaller ships were captured off Lyme; one carrying arms and powder for 5,000 men. At Sedgemoor the powder ran out.

Two Somerset Girls: The first account is probably true but not documented. A good theme for an opera. The sword given to Mary Bridges is in Taunton Museum.

Bridgwater: Once a thriving port, its port facilities have ceased. To have a town so far up a dangerous river may seem odd, but there are on the Somerset coast few other facilities apart from Watchet and Minehead. The river was a defensive system, and if you judged the bore right it could work to your advantage. It is really only the size of vessels which have made Bridgwater redundant; that and the railway and the M5. Bristol now has Avonmouth, and Bridgwater only has Dunball Wharf. However, at Combwich there have been some suspiciously large advances. Old women mention Hinkley under their breath and shake their heads. Bridgwater, once the bridge was built, ensured that there was a monopoly of barge traffic betwen there and Langport. All goods had to be unloaded onto smaller vessels. The bridge part of Bridgwater was no less important than the docks, though its name derives actually from one Walter of Douai. It should be Bridge-Walter. Others favour the Old English 'brycg' meaning gangplank or Old Norse 'bryggja' meaning jetty or quay. See 'Bridgwater' by Robert Dunning. Bricks, tiles and glass added to the town's skills. More recently it has been plastics, British Cellophane and bin liners, as well as the so-called 'secret' munitions factory at Puriton. The wharf at Dunball still works, but only just. Bridgwater is well worth a visit, home to the carnival, Blake and the painting in the church, to say nothing of slime batches and Bath bricks, which were exported all over the world. The siege of Bridgwater was brief. History does not relate what happened to the spirited Christabella. Not only was she wetnurse to the future king, Charles II, but is reputed to have seduced him on his sixteenth birthday. The young Charles II was born in 1630 so he would only have been 15 at the time of the siege... There is still a pub called the Wyndham Arms in Kingsbury Episcopi, where the family owned land until the 1950's.

Albert Street Cutting: This is about a very different stretch of water, but in its time just as important. The canal which took traffic from Bridgwater docks right through to Firepool Weir in Taunton, was constructed in the 1820's but was superseded by the railway in the 1840's. Albert Street Cutting is a deep cut on the western side of Bridgwater, with large timber baulks bolstering the two walls. It looks like some mediaeval moat, which is pretty well what it is. The brickwork on some of the bridges is magnificent and it doesn't take much to imagine what it must have been like with horsedrawn traffic.

Overheard in a Bridgwater Kitchen Late One Night: Just read it fast, and with the right intonations of an irate father.

The Explosives Factory: No comment, except that the Royal Ordnance Factory is now privatised and owned by British Aerospace. They not only make high grade explosive but also process sulphuric acid. They are apparently putting in a reed bed to process some of their nastier chemicals which have been known to slip into the ditches. Stories abound of various goings on in the past... Only now are the inspectors from the Environmental Agency allowed in. For fifty years the factory has been immune from the normal environmental controls. There is however a new approach and openness which will be welcomed by all. For an article on wildlife in the factory see 'Surprises at the Royal Ordnance' by Trevor Freeston in the July '96 issue of The Somerset Magazine. In the phone book, Royal Ordnance Plc is sandwiched between thirteen Royal Oaks and the RSPCA.

Spuddling around Burtle, Shapwick, Catcott and Ashcott: Heavy industry indeed. The mountains of peat contrast dramatically with the flatness and neatness of the machine cut blocks. Great wealth for those that own the land, not a place to put your car or lorry off the road into a ditch. I like the wild feel of the Levels here, like the outback. Around Ashcott there is even a road sign saying deformed road, and driving along it is like turbulence in an aircraft.

Ancient Trackways: These trackways, of which there are quite a few that have been excavated, show a varying degree of sophistication. Some are merely brushwood thrown down, others are hurdles, and some are plank walkways with pile. All are very old and must have connected villages either with each other or to the dry land in winter. The archaeology of Somerset is fascinating and well worth investigating. Peat preserves all sorts of things that would otherwise have disappeared; pollen, cloth, bone, wood, etc. The best known track is perhaps the Sweet Track but there are many others; the Eclipse, Tinneys, Abbots Way. No doubt others have been dug up in the past without realising what they were; the earliest tracks in Europe. I once met a woman at Burrow Hill buying cider for her grandfather who was 102. He had started work in Taunton in the 1890's, aged six, holding the horses when they changed them for the stage coach from Bristol to Exeter. Now we have the M5, all in one lifetime.

Peat Cutting: Not much peat is cut by hand, but in the past everything had to be cut out and dried, in hyles and then ruckles. Slabs of peat cut in Somerset were larger than elsewhere but then split down into three. It was only the blacksmith who used coal, although on Dartmoor there has been some evidence of peat being treated to form a kind of charcoal which could give higher temperatures for smelting. Most of today's peat goes for gardens and there may come a time when peat cutting will have to stop altogether for environmental reasons. The Somerset peat does not regenerate and it is a finite resource, though the conditions are still wet enough in some areas around Burtle. Getting the peat dry was always a problem. I have seen peat cut on Dartmoor in the sixties and I have cut it myself in the Outer Hebrides. The smell of good peat burning is incomparable. How long commercial peatcutting will go on for, is debatable. Peatlands in Southern England are a rare ecological resource. Peat was the poor man's coal. Now we have oil...

Water Hanging: Again self evident, but it does take a very long time for the water to completely drain away and the patchwork effect is very striking when the floods are about three quarters diminished. The secret is to let the heavy water lie for long enough to deposit its silt which replenishes the soil, but not too long that it kills the grass. Pumping stations have been known to only work in off peak times, but the capacities of various pumps have been improved. For a more detailed look at what the NRA is doing, there is a consultation document called 'Somerset Moors and Levels Studies', drawn up in June 1995 by Ken Tatem which is very informative. The NRA is now called The Environment Agency, and is responsible for monitoring air and land pollution as well as water.

Stogursey Castle: Slightly off the route but a delightful castle with a moat. The family that owned Stogursey also owned a lot of the land and the coastal rights for fishing. No doubt they wish that they had feudal rights to nuclear power.

Combwich, Steart, The Sea: Visit this place on a cold winter's day in a storm and you will experience the elements in their true ferociousness. There was once a plan to bypass the Parrett Estuary and cut through the Steart Peninsular. This was put forward in 1723. A smaller bypass had been cut near Dunball in 1677-8, which was very successful and cut off a large loop known as Viking's Pill. The second scheme was never implemented for several reasons, but it would have cut six miles off the journey to Bridgwater and enabled shipping to get up there in one tide. There were other advantages, not only with the drainage but with the new land created, but the uncertainties about tidal flooding of Bridgwater, and the creation of a natural bar at the mouth, caused the proposers to err on the side of caution. In 1824 another scheme was put forward by Thomas Telford to have a port at Stolford and use it as the terminus of the canal system which would run from Beer on the south coast. He had just finished the Caledonian Canal in Scotland and was on a high. To make the connection across the South West was ambitious and costly. It never got built. Steam ships had made their appearance and their added size and safety around Land's End made the project look less advantageous. The prospect of Hinkley on the horizon dominates the area both physically and psychologically. When Hinkley was first built Combwich was still on diesel generators. This powerstation was known as the 'bomb' factory, and residents were promised 'free' electricity. 'Steart' is a mediaeval word meaning the tail of an animal, or spur, both of which are applicable,

Hinkley Point: There are in fact four reactors at Hinkley; two in Hinkley A, the old Magnox reactors which are now over 30 years old and near the end of their life; and the two Advanced Gas Cooled Reactors in Hinkley B, which are now at least 25 years old. Large scale local opposition has prevented the building of Hinkley C, a planned Pressurised Water Reactor. This plan was eventually turned down at a public enquiry in 1989. The recent construction of a new wharf and port facilities at Combwich has raised more questions than answers.

Hinkley is a large employer, but with privatisation and the fact that the reactors are being worked well beyond their predicted 'sell by' dates, means that the nuclear industry in Somerset is perhaps entering its most unpredictable phase. George and I went round on a Friday. The next Tuesday, only hours after the bids for privatisation were in, they announced the shutting down of the other Hinkley B reactor, due to the search for cracks in the welds. For a good synopsis of the nuclear debate see Crispin Aubrey's book 'Meltdown: The Collapse of the Nuclear Dream'. Tacky shades are a common sight up and down the Severn Estuary, and are perioically tested for 'nuclear' dust.

Mud-Horsemen: Brendan Sellick and his sons are the last active mud-horsemen fishing off Stolford. Their method of fishing has changed little since neolithic times. Nets strung out on poles. The modern nets are probably better and mended more easily, but it is still a long haul out there and back. The mud-horse is a sledge with a curved front which is pushed out, and then brought back to help carry the catch. They also help to spread the load over the mud which can be treacherous. The tides come in very quickly and you have to know what you are doing. Cheaper than a trawler, radar and echo sounder, radio and massive nets, it is ecologically sound, as a man can only bring back what he can carry. It is however in the shadow of Hinkley Point nuclear power station, accused of drawing in all manner of fish and small sea creatures through its sea cooling system. Brendan estimates that the shrimp population has decreased to 10 percent of what it was forty years ago. There was an eel farm in the warmer cooling waters but that was stopped suddenly for reasons which were not clear. The water cooling system draws in one million gallons a minute and this is returned to the sea about 15°C warmer. This is a vast quantity of water, and at that rate would drain the Bristol Channel in a week. The fish caught up in the system are just spread on the land or taken away and used as fishmeal for garden centres. A great waste. 'How much' is open to debate. Some say 8 tons a year, some say as much as a trawler, but that's a trawler close to the shore. To try and reduce this they experimented with ultrasound two years ago, but without much success. The term 'mud-horse' may come from the fact that feudal rights extended as far out as the Lord of the Manor could ride his horse. Brendan is concerned about the young fish and the long term effects on the breeding grounds. Even the mud has shifted.

Look at the Stream: This quote comes from 'Blood Earth & Medicine' and is carved into a bridge at the new Bishop Fox's School in Taunton. The letter cutting and design is by Richard Kindersley and he has allowed me to reproduce his photograph of it here as an example of his work.

Pigeon Biter

James Crowden

James was born in 1954, travelled widely in the Middle East and spent a winter in the Himalayas on his own. After a brief spell studying civil engineering and anthropology he settled in Dorset where he took up sheep shearing, lambing, forestry and cidermaking as a way of life. He moved to Somerset in 1986. His first book of poetry 'Blood Earth & Medicine', highlighting the year of a casual agricultural labourer, was published in 1991. This was adapted for performance and radio.

George Wright

George studied Graphic Design at Wimbledon School of Art. He works as a freelance photographer for books and magazines including The Independent, Observer and Telegraph. He recently photographed the last journey of Michael Rockefeller who disappeared in the jungles of Irian Jaya. When not travelling the globe, George lives in a remote farmhouse in West Dorset, not far from the source of the Parrett.

Selected Bibliography

The Drainage of the Somerset Levels: Michael Williams, CUP, 1970.

The Natural History of the Somerset Levels: Bernard Storer, Second Edition, Dovecote Press, 1985.

Wetland: Life in the Somerset Levels: Patrick Sutherland & Adam Nicholson, Mermaid Books, 1986.

Secrets of the Levels: Chris Chapman, Somerset Books, 1996.

Avalon & Sedgemoor: Desmond Hawkins, Alan Sutton, 1982.

Somerset Levels and Moors: Ken Fletcher, Somerset County Council, 1991.

The Somerset Levels: Robin and Romey Williams, Ex Libris Press, 1992.

Bridgwater: Robert Dunning, Alan Sutton, 1992.

The Monmouth Rebellion: Robert Dunning, Dovecote Press, 1984.

A History of Somerset: Robert Dunning, Phillimore & Co, 1983.

Somerset & Avon: Robert Dunning, Bartholemew and Son, 1980; Revised Edition, Alan Sutton, 1992.

The Dorset & Somerset Rebellion: K Merle Chacksfield, The Dorset Publishing Company, 1985.

Bridgwater Docks and the River Parrett: Brian Murless, Somerset County Council Library Service, 1983.

Bridgwater & The River Parrett Old Photographs: Compiled by Rod Fitzhugh, Alan Sutton, 1993.

By Waterway to Taunton: The History of the Bridgwater & Taunton Canal: Tony Haskell, Somerset Books, 1994.

"...Bogs and inundations...": Iain Miles, Somerset Industrial Archaeological Society.

The Archaeology of Somerset: Michael Aston & Ian Barrow, Somerset County Council, 1982.

Aspects of the Mediaeval Landscape of Somerset: Michael Aston, Somerset County Council, 1988.

The Lake Villages of Somerset: Minnitt and Coles, Somerset Levels Project, 1996.

Prehistory of the Somerset Levels: JM and BJ Coles, Somerset Levels Project, 1989.

The Bond of Green Withy: Berta Lawrence, Werner Laurie, 1954.

The Levels: Peter Benson, Constable, 1987.

Langport: Heather Ridgway, Wessex House Press, 1994.

Meltdown: The Collapse of the Nuclear Dream: Crispin Aubrey, Collins & Brown, 1991.

Somerset: Chris Willoughby, Alan Sutton, 1993.

Muchelney Memoranda: A breviary of the Abbey: B Scholfield, 1927.